Prayers of Freedom

A Collection of Prayers
For Deliverance and Healing
Organized by Topic

"The Spirit of the Lord is upon Me,
Because He has anointed Me to bring
good news to the poor.
He has sent Me to proclaim release to captives,
And recovery of sight to the blind,
To set free those who are oppressed,"
~ Jesus (Luke 4:18)

Scripture quotations labelled KJV are taken from the King James Version of the Bible

Some Prayer guideline quotations are taken from the resource pages of Jubilee Resources International Inc.
PO Box 3, Feilding 4740, New Zealand
www.JubileeResources.org © Selwyn R. Stevens, 1994, 1996, 1999, 2004, 2007, 2015, 2017 Used by permission. All Rights Reserved.

Printed in the United States of America

Free Range Family Ministries
www.FreeRangeFamily.org

First Edition: April 2024

ISBN: 9798322717416
Independently published

Introduction

The following book is a list of prayers that is meant to be used as a tool to help people in the process of understanding and receiving the total freedom in Jesus Christ (Yeshua Hamashiach) that is available to them.

You will see scripture quoted all throughout this book, because first and foremost we need to look to the Word of God and Revelation of the Holy Spirit for instruction. In addition to scripture, you will see practical tips and tools to aid in receiving and ministering deliverance. Just like any other type of ministry such as healing, intercessory prayer, teaching, pastoring, etc., we can glean from the wisdom of those who have decades of experience doing the work in a ministry that has shown good fruit.

In no way should this book be treated as a special formula to be set free. In fact, you could say every prayer in this book and nothing would happen if you weren't truly repentant in your heart and exercising true faith in Jesus Christ. It is only by His power that we are set free and just like other miracles of physical healing, baptism in the Holy Spirit, etc. deliverance can look different for every person according to how the Lord wants to do it in them for His glory.

I used to avoid any type of repeat after me or written prayer until the Lord showed me that they have a time and place when they assist us in knowing what to pray about a certain subject. The Lord has a way of changing my mind and He did that as He supernaturally healed me as I prayed a written prayer that I otherwise would not have known to pray had I not seen it in a book. I've also noticed that they can be especially helpful for people who want to pray powerfully, but may have trouble coming up with words right on the spot.

The hang up however is the temptation for some to just read the words on a paper and think they prayed when in reality their mind was wandering and they weren't truly meaning what they were saying in their heart. This can easily turn into babbling on and on like the pagans do thinking that they will be heard for their many words. (Matthew 6:7)

It is my recommendation that you use these prayers only as guidelines to assist you. Always be led by the Holy Spirit directly as far as which ones to pray and how. Continually examine yourself to see if you are starting to just ritually read a prayer instead of praying it from your heart, and if you fall into that, stop and change it to your own words.

One thing to be aware of that I've personally seen, is there can be spiritual resistance to people praying written prayers, because they are powerful. They are straight forward and follow the instructions given to us in scripture. Sometimes the resistance that someone feels toward praying a written prayer is from the enemy. The spirit that doesn't want to leave a person convinces them not to pray the prayer laid out for them, but to only pray in their "own words". I've then watched as the person starts to pray a very long and powerless prayer of complaining and babbling and talking in circles. Sometimes what they were saying didn't even make sense. I've recognized that this is actually a demonic manifestation to fool someone into just talking in circles instead of confession, repentance, and casting out the spirit. So as you can see the risk of babbling like a pagan can be seen in both reading prayers and refusing to read them. Ask the Lord for discernment in this area to guide you so that your prayers are effective and powerful, not religious and weak. My favorite is when people think it's completely silly to read a prayer, but they do it just to humor me and before they're even 3 lines in, they are weeping and being touched by the power of God as He delivers them, and heals them of things they didn't even know they needed to be set free of. Praise the Lord!

I recommend that you pause throughout your prayers to ask the Lord what else to say or pray and if there is anything practical that He wants you to do in faith to experience total freedom from what you are praying about. This might include forgiving someone or confessing something to someone, or getting rid of something that is in your possession. Trust in the Lord and His plan for you. Wait on Him and He will answer you and guide you.

When it comes to deliverance, there are two lies that the enemy (or his minions) will try to fool people into believing. 1) He will want you to believe you are already free when you are not, because you won't pray in repentance and cast out what you don't believe is there. 2) He (and his minions) will also try to convince you that you are not free and forgiven when you really are. Most people report having to fight off lies of the enemy shortly after they are delivered, saying "you are not really free." and "That wasn't real." Do not believe them. Stand in faith and confess that you are free unless the Holy Spirit confirms that there is something still to deal with. Whenever we listen to the voice of the enemy we open the door to his destruction. We must only listen to the voice of the Lord and do what the Holy spirit reveals to us. If you have already confessed a sin or prayed a prayer of repentance in this book, there is no need to keep confessing or praying the same thing over and over again.

The only time we should ever repeat a prayer is if we happen to fall into that same sin and need to repent and it should be a quick "nail it to the cross" moment and then move on. If you find yourself praying a prayer of repentance and falling into that same sin repeatedly you need to deeply seek the Lord for revelation on why this is still an issue in your life. Did you truly address the right spirit, break its legal right to be in your life and boldly tell it to go until it actually left? Is more prayer and fasting necessary for this deliverance? Were you truly praying in repentance of this sin or were you just looking for quick relief from the consequences of torment it caused without actually wanting to turn from it? Are there wounds in your soul that you need the Lord to heal? Is there something you are doing that is deceiving you into opening the door back up to the enemy again? These are all questions that you might want to consider praying about with the Lord. We will touch on some of these hindrances to deliverance in the first part of this prayer book. Remember, the Lord knows your heart and He isn't just interested in you being free for a moment, He is interested in you continually walking in freedom and being able to minister that same freedom in Jesus Christ to others.

Matthew 10:8
Heal the sick, raise the dead, cleanse those with leprosy, cast out demons. Freely you received, freely give.

TABLE OF CONTENTS

BIBLICAL BASIS FOR DELIVERANCE......................1

    CONFESSION 8

    REPENTANCE AND RENOUNCEMENT 10

    SIN AND UNFORGIVENESS 12

    BLESSING AND CURSING..................................... 15

    CAN A CHRISTIAN HAVE DEMONS? 31

    SPIRITUAL WARFARE... 38

    THE DELIVERANCE MINISTRY OF JESUS........................ 41

    DELIVERANCE MINISTRY OF BELIEVERS 42

    DO YOU HAVE POWER AND AUTHORITY IN CHRIST?.. 44

OPENING PRAYERS... 47

    PRAYER OF SALVATION IN JESUS CHRIST...................... 47

    TAKING AUTHORITY.. 49

HINDRANCES TO DELIVERANCE 51

    FEAR 51

    PRIDE AND REBELLION....................................... 54

    INSINCERE REPENTANCE 56

    DOUBT AND UNBELIEF 57

    UNFORGIVENESS 59

    GENERAL PRAYER TO BREAK OFF HINDRANCES 63

HEARING THE VOICE OF GOD............................. 65

    SCRIPTURES ABOUT HEARING GOD 67

    REMOVING HINDRANCES TO HEARING GOD 72

RENOUNCEMENT PRAYERS BY TOPIC 77

OCCULT / WITCHCRAFT.. 79

INVOLVEMENT IN SATANISM 85

SECRET SOCIETIES 90

INVOLVEMENT IN RELIGIONS 96

REIKI & OTHER QUESTIONABLE PRACTICES 107

MODERN / WESTERN MEDICINE.................................. 114

REJECTION... 120

GUILT AND SHAME.. 127

ANGER.. 129

ABUSE 131

DEPRESSION 134

ANXIETY.. 137

PERFORMANCE / PERFECTIONISM............................... 141

SEXUAL ISSUES 144

    List of Sexual sins / open doors.............................. 153

    Adultery/Fornication 157

    Sexual Power and Deception 159

    Molestation Rape Incest 160

    Homosexuality.. 162

    Sexual Identity 164

    Divorce.. 166

    Miscarriages.. 168

SOUL TIES... 170

HARMING SELF OR OTHERS... 173

    Addictions / Substance Abuse................................. 174

    Shedding of innocent blood..................................... 176

    Eating Disorders 179

    Cutting / Other Self Harm 181

    Suicidal Tendencies 182

    Racism / Chauvinism... 183

    Mistreatment of People Groups 185

    Gossip / Slander / Word Curses 188

WORD CURSES.. 190

PRONOUNCEMENTS... 191

LIES OF THE ENEMY 192

VOWS 196

LEGALISM 198

NOT HONORING YOUR FATHER AND MOTHER.......... 199

FINANCIAL STRONGHOLDS.. 200

GENERAL RENOUNCEMENT PRAYERS 204

INVOLVEMENT IN QUESTIONABLE THINGS................. 205

ACTIVE CURSES / WITCHCRAFT 206

BREAKING GENERATIONAL CURSES 207

RELEASING GENERATIONAL BLESSING 213

EXAMPLES OF SPIRITS 217

COMMON NAMES/FUNCTIONS 224

LEVIATHAN.. 226

ABADDON / APOLLYON.. 229

JEZEBEL 231

DEATH... 239

INFIRMITY 241

EXTRA HELP AND PRAYERS 243

JEWISH PARTICIPANTS... 244

THE TRUTH ABOUT OUR HEAVENLY FATHER 244

CLEANSING & BLESSING HOME AND LAND 248

Biblical Basis for Deliverance

To understand deliverance, we must understand the legality of scripture. The Bible is filled with legal terms. Demons can't freely terrorize whoever they want. There has to be some sort of legal reason for them to be in someone's life. Many Christians will only read the parts of scripture that are easy to understand and feel okay with. Many don't even go outside the New Testament because they believe that things in the Old Testament don't apply to them anymore. This has led to an ignorance in the Christian faith about deliverance and I believe that has been the enemy's plan all along. You will not address and break the power of something that you do not believe exists. Only when we read the entirety of scripture, is when we can fully understand the power of Jesus and what he did for us on the cross. When we read the parts of scripture that make us uncomfortable, we are forced to learn about the rights the enemy may have in our life, and how to come out of agreement with Him to fully receive the fullness of salvation that our Messiah paid the price for. Sometimes we need to get outside of our western mindset and read scripture in the Hebraic way that it was written. This means looking past the simple logical meaning of black words on white paper, and understanding it as the Living Word that it is, full of types, shadows, prophecy, and imagery that is there for us to search out matters and gain deeper understanding. I also recommend using tools to study the Hebrew and Greek words that are used in scripture and what they mean. You will find that so much can be lost in translation. After studying this way for years, I've realized that it's no wonder our society has moved away from true deliverance and healing because much of what Ive learned had come from the original Greek and Hebrew and most Christians in America don't even read their English Bibles, not to mention, study them in their original languages. Reading scripture in this way really helps us further understand our role in walking out our salvation and the freedom that is available to us.

An example of this is the following passage from James:

James 5:13-18 NASBS

Is anyone among you suffering? Then he must pray. Is anyone cheerful? He is to sing praises. [14] Is anyone among you sick? Then he must call for the elders of the church and they are to pray over him, anointing him with oil in the name of the Lord; [15] and the prayer offered in faith will restore the one who is sick, and the Lord will raise him up, and if he has committed sins, they will be forgiven him. [16] Therefore, confess your sins to one another, and pray for one another so that you may be healed. The effective prayer of a righteous man can accomplish much. [17] Elijah was a man with a nature like ours, and he prayed earnestly that it would not rain, and it did not rain on the earth for three years and six months. [18] Then he prayed again, and the sky poured rain and the earth produced its fruit.

When I just used to read this is the simple English translation, I thought this passage only referred to someone who was physically ill and needed physical healing in their body, but the Lord encouraged me to dig deeper and study it more closely.

I looked up the Greek word translated as sick. It is the Greek word astheneō. According to Thayer's Definition this word can mean "to be

weak, feeble, to be without strength, powerless."
It also means "to be weak in means, needy, poor."

Then I looked up the Greek word for the second
time the English word sick was mentioned and it
was a different word, kamnō. According to
Strong's and Thayer's definitions, this word
means to toil or to tire, to grow weary, or be
weary. This would be more like when we say we
are so sick and tired of something that we've been
dealing with unsuccessfully for so long.

And the next word I studied was one of my
favorite words in all of Scripture. The word
translated here as restore, is the Greek word sōzō.
According to Strong's Definition this means to
save, deliver or protect (literally or figuratively): -
to heal, preserve, save, do well be (make) whole.
Thayer's Definition is to save, keep safe and
sound - to rescue from danger or destruction
(from injury or peril) - to save a suffering one
(from perishing) - to preserve one who is in
danger of destruction, to save or rescue - to save
in the technical biblical sense - to deliver from the
penalties of the Messianic judgment - to save
from the evils which obstruct the reception of the
Messianic deliverance

Then we come down to the word healed and that is the Greek word "iaomai." This means to cure, heal, make whole, to free from errors and sins, or to bring about one's salvation.

So if we replace some of these English words with the definitions of the Greek words they represent this passage might read very differently.

James 5:13-18 NASBS
Is anyone among you suffering? Then he must pray. Is anyone cheerful? He is to sing praises. [14] Is anyone among you *weak or in need of something*? Then he must call for the elders of the church and they are to pray over him, anointing him with oil in the name of the Lord; [15] and the prayer offered in faith will *deliver* the one who is *weary from toil, from all hindrances obstructing them from receiving everything that Jesus paid for*, and the Lord will raise him up, and if he has committed sins, they will be forgiven him. [16] Therefore, confess your sins to one another, and pray for one another so that you may be *healed, whole, and free from the effects of sin*. The effective prayer of a righteous man can accomplish much. [17] Elijah was a man with a nature like ours, and he prayed earnestly that it would not rain, and it did not rain on the earth for three years and six months. [18] Then he prayed again, and the

sky poured rain and the earth produced its fruit.

Even though Jesus fully paid the price for our deliverance, there can be things like unrepentant sin, unforgiveness, agreement with lies of the enemy, word curses, vows we've made, etc., that can obstruct our ability to fully receive the sōzō kind of salvation, of full deliverance and healing that we have access to.

Throughout this book you will see a mention of closing the door on the enemy. In Genesis, before Cain killed Abel, the Lord warns him, "…sin is crouching at the door; and its desire is for you, but you must master it." Sin will always be looking for a way in. 1 Peter 5:8 tells us that Satan, our adversary, the devil, "prowls around like a roaring lion, seeking someone to devour." Ephesians 4:27 tells us not to give place to the devil. That word for place is the Greek word "topos" which actually means a physical place to occupy.

It is my hope that with the guidance of the Holy Spirit, this book will help serve as a guideline to help you pray through different issues by the leading of the Holy Spirit and break any legal ground the enemy has used to try to hinder you from walking in total freedom.

Without focusing too much on demons and demonology, I hope this book gives you enough background that you can better understand how to use the power and authority you have in Jesus Christ and the discernment given to you by the Holy Spirit to cast out every evil spirit from your life. I also believe that this book will be a tool to help you make sure that even if you are not specifically dealing with an evil spirit or struggling in a particular area that all legal ground is broken and every door to your life is closed to the enemy, so that when he or his minions do come to try to find a place in your life whether through your own sin, the sin of your ancestors, unforgiveness, trauma, etc., they simply can't find a way in and have to flee from you and your family.

My hope as you walk out your freedom in Jesus Christ is that you grow in your discernment without giving place to fear; and that you grow in your faith, without giving place to ignorance. My advice to you would be to make sure you stay in the balance of recognizing that there may be something spiritual going on, without making your focus on the enemy and demons all the time.

Stay focused on Jesus and His mighty power. Listen to the voice of the Holy Spirit and only address evil or pain and trauma when you believe the Lord is directing you to do so. Many times, people will find an extreme when they should be in balance. There are always going to be Christians in the "faith" camp totally ignoring their need for deliverance, and the Christians in the "deliverance" camp paying attention to the enemy and what his demons are doing more than the power of God. Balance is necessary and can be attained through wisdom and discernment from the Word of God, and the Holy Spirit guiding us.

The following are descriptions of terms as well as scriptures we can study about the various topics surrounding deliverance.

Confession

Confession is the formal statement that we give admitting that we have sinned and need forgiveness. In scripture, we see this done not only on behalf of one's self, but also their ancestors.

1 John 1:8-9 ESV

If we claim to be without sin, we deceive ourselves and the truth is not in us. If we confess our sins, he is faithful and just and will forgive us our sins and purify us from all unrighteousness.

James 5:16

Therefore, confess your sins to one another, and pray for one another so that you may be healed. A prayer of a righteous person, when it is brought about, can accomplish much.

Leviticus 26:40-42

'But if they confess their wrongdoing and the wrongdoing of their forefathers, in their unfaithfulness which they committed against Me, and also in their acting with hostility against Me— 41 I also was acting with hostility against them, to bring them into the land of their enemies—or if their uncircumcised heart is humbled so that they then make amends for their wrongdoing, 42 then I will remember My covenant with Jacob, and I will remember also My covenant with Isaac, and My covenant with Abraham as well, and I will remember the land.

Nehemiah 9:2

The descendants of Israel separated themselves from all foreigners, and they stood and confessed their sins and the wrongdoings of their fathers.

There is no way in the natural that we can go through and remember every single sin the we or our ancestors committed, and I do not recommend, but the Lord can reveal to us by the power of the holy spirit everything that we need to address and come out of agreement with to walk in freedom. This may take time and waiting on the Lord. He may require you to fast, ask someone for forgiveness, forgive someone who hurt you, confess your sin out loud to someone, ask someone to pray for you, etc. I don't know exactly what the Lord will guide you to do, but I do know that if you obey Him, it will be totally worth it.

Repentance and Renouncement

To repent and renounce something is to come out of agreement with and totally turn from it. This can be the sin that we or our ancestors have committed, the lies of the enemy that we've believed, etc.

2 Corinthians 4:2

2 but we have renounced the things hidden because of shame, not walking in trickery nor distorting the word of God, but by the open proclamation of the truth commending ourselves to every person's conscience in the sight of God.

2 Timothy 2:19 NLT
19 But God's truth stands firm like a foundation stone with this inscription: "The Lord knows those who are his," and "All who belong to the Lord must turn away from evil."

Titus 2:11-13
11 For the grace of God has appeared, bringing salvation to all people, 12 instructing us to deny ungodliness and worldly desires and to live sensibly, righteously, and in a godly manner in the present age, 13 looking for the blessed hope and the appearing of the glory of our great God and Savior, Christ Jesus,

Revelation 3:19
Those whom I love, I rebuke and discipline; therefore, be zealous and repent.

2 Chronicles 7:13-14
13 If I shut up the heavens so that there is no rain, or if I command the locust to devour the land, or if I send a plague among My

people, 14 and My people who are called by My name humble themselves, and pray and seek My face, and turn from their wicked ways, then I will hear from heaven, and I will forgive their sin and will heal their land.

Proverbs 28:13 ESV
Whoever conceals their sins does not prosper, but the one who confesses and renounces them finds mercy.

Sin and Unforgiveness

Jesus has paid the price for our freedom and healing. His death and resurrection on the cross is enough to break curses, forgive our sins, and heal us. However, hindrances like unrepentant sin and unforgiveness can get in the way of us walking in the total freedom that Jesus offers to us.

I've heard it said at some altar calls that Jesus' death and resurrection means that every one of us is already forgiven of all of our sins past present and future and repentance isn't necessary, but that's not what I see in the word of God. Let's look at what scripture says about this.

Matthew 6:14-15

14 For if you forgive other people for their offenses *(wrongdoings)*, your heavenly Father will also forgive you. 15 But if you do not forgive other people, then your Father will not forgive your offenses *(wrongdoings)*.

2 Corinthians 2:9-11
9 For to this end I also wrote, so that I might put you to the test, whether you are obedient in all things. 10 But one whom you forgive anything, I also forgive; for indeed what I have forgiven, if I have forgiven anything, I did so for your sakes in the presence of Christ, 11 so that no advantage would be taken of us by Satan, for we are not ignorant of his schemes.

Matthew 18:23-35
23 "For this reason the kingdom of heaven is like a king who wanted to settle accounts with his slaves. 24 And when he had begun to settle them, one who owed him ten thousand talents was brought to him. 25 But since he did not have the means to repay, his master commanded that he be sold, along with his wife and children and all that he had, and repayment be made. 26 So the slave fell to the ground and prostrated himself before him, saying, 'Have patience with me and I will repay you everything.' 27 And the master of that slave felt compassion, and he released him and forgave him the debt. 28 But that

slave went out and found one of his fellow slaves who owed him a hundred denarii; and he seized him and began to choke him, saying, 'Pay back what you owe!' 29 So his fellow slave fell to the ground and began to plead with him, saying, 'Have patience with me and I will repay you.' 30 But he was unwilling, and went and threw him in prison until he would pay back what was owed. 31 So when his fellow slaves saw what had happened, they were deeply grieved and came and reported to their master all that had happened. 32 Then summoning him, his master *said to him, 'You wicked slave, I forgave you all that debt because you pleaded with me. 33 Should you not also have had mercy on your fellow slave, in the same way that I had mercy on you?' 34 And his master, moved with anger, handed him over to the torturers until he would repay all that was owed him. 35 My heavenly Father will also do the same to you, if each of you does not forgive his brother from your heart."

Isaiah 59:1-2
Behold, the Lord's hand is not shortened, that it cannot save; nor His ear heavy, that it cannot hear. But your iniquities have separated you from your God and your sins have hidden His face from you, so that He will not hear.

John 5:14-15

14 Afterward, Jesus found him in the temple and said to him, "Behold, you have become well; do not sin anymore, so that nothing worse happens to you." 15 The man went away, and informed the Jews that it was Jesus who had made him well.

Ephesians 4:26-27 NKJV

26 "Be angry, and do not sin": do not let the sun go down on your wrath, 27 nor give place to the devil.

Blessing and Cursing

Many Christians have a hard time facing the fact that they may be under a curse that needs to be broken. If I didn't have this personally happen in my life in such a radical way it might be hard for me to grasp as well, but since then I have studied the scriptures to learn what they say about curses and blessings, so that I can have substantial Biblical evidence for what happened in my life and so many others who we have ministered to.

The first question I would ask someone who says curses don't exist anymore, or that Christians can't be under a curse is. "Then why do we die?" Man was originally created to live forever until the curse that Adam and Eve brought by their sin. This is a curse that has existed since that time in the Garden of Eden and based on what I've read in scripture, will continue until the second coming of the Lord and the New Jerusalem.

> 11 People will live in it, and there will no longer be a curse, for Jerusalem will dwell in security.
> Zechariah 14:11

> 1 Then he showed me a river of the water of life, clear as crystal, coming from the throne of God and of the Lamb, 2 in the middle of its street. On either side of the river was the tree of life, bearing twelve kinds of fruit, yielding its fruit every month; and the leaves of the tree were for the healing of the nations. 3 There will no longer be any curse; and the throne of God and of the Lamb will be in it, and His bond-servants will serve Him; 4 they will see His face, and His name will be on their foreheads. 5 And there will no longer be any night; and they will not have need of the light of a lamp nor the light of the sun, because the Lord God will illumine them; and they will reign forever and ever.
> Revelation 22:1-5 NASB

First let's look at the word "curse" and how it's used in the context of scripture:

Genesis 3:14

The Lord God said to the serpent, "Because you have done this, Cursed are you more than all cattle, And more than every beast of the field; On your belly you will go,

And dust you will eat; All the days of your life;

Genesis 3:17-19 NASB

17 Then to Adam He said, "Because you have listened to the voice of your wife, and have eaten from the tree about which I commanded you, saying, 'You shall not eat from it'; Cursed is the ground because of you; In toil you will eat of it All the days of your life.

18 "Both thorns and thistles it shall grow for you; And you will eat the plants of the field;

19 By the sweat of your face You will eat bread,

Till you return to the ground, Because from it you were taken; For you are dust, And to dust you shall return."

Genesis 12:2-4 NASB

2 And I will make you a great nation,

And I will bless you,

And make your name great;

And so you shall be a blessing;

3 And I will bless those who bless you,

And the one who curses you I will curse.
And in you all the families of the earth will be blessed."
4 So Abram went forth as the Lord had spoken to him; and Lot went with him. Now Abram was seventy-five years old when he departed from Haran.

Deuteronomy 11:26-28
26 "See, I am setting before you today a blessing and a curse: 27 the blessing, if you listen to the commandments of the Lord your God, which I am commanding you today; 28 and the curse, if you do not listen to the commandments of the Lord your God, but turn aside from the way which I am commanding you today, by following other gods which you have not known.

Deuteronomy 30:19
19 I call heaven and earth to witness against you today, that I have set before you life and death, the blessing and the curse. So choose life in order that you may live, you and your descendants, 20 by loving the Lord your God, by obeying His voice, and by holding fast to Him;

Proverbs 3:33
The curse of the Lord is on the house of the wicked,
But He blesses the dwelling of the righteous.

Proverbs 28:27
He who gives to the poor will never want,
But he who shuts his eyes will have many curses.

Malachi 2:2
2 If you do not listen, and if you do not take
it to heart to give honor to My name," says
the Lord of hosts, "then I will send the curse
upon you and I will curse your blessings; and
indeed, I have cursed them already, because
you are not taking it to heart.

Malachi 3:8-12
8 "Will a man rob God? Yet you are robbing
Me! But you say, 'How have we robbed You?'
In tithes and offerings. 9 You are cursed with
a curse, for you are robbing Me, the whole
nation of you! 10 Bring the whole tithe into
the storehouse, so that there may be food in
My house, and test Me now in this," says the
Lord of hosts, "if I will not open for you the
windows of heaven and pour out for you a
blessing until it overflows. 11 Then I will
rebuke the devourer for you, so that it will
not destroy the fruits of the ground; nor will
your vine in the field cast its grapes," says the
Lord of hosts. 12 "All the nations will call
you blessed, for you shall be a delightful
land," says the Lord of hosts.

Perhaps the largest area of scripture where we see the difference between blessing and cursing is in Deuteronomy 28. I don't have the room in this book to include it all but I suggest that you go look it up and study what God's word says here. Many people want to quote Deuteronomy 28:1-14, but they don't go near Deuteronomy 28:15-68. They also want to claim the blessings in the beginning of Deuteronomy 28 but forget to acknowledge that it says those blessing are for those to obey the Lord and do what He commands.

To understand Blessing and Cursing we must understand to duality of scripture. Just like there is no good without the existence of evil, and no light without the existence of darkness, there is no blessing without the existence of curses.

Is there such thing as generational curses?

The Bible doesn't necessarily say the exact term "generational curses" but it does talk about curses and we can see the consequences of curses that have come down generationally all throughout scripture. Another term that might be more accurate would be "generational iniquity" or "generational punishment."

What does the Bible say about generational curses, iniquity or punishment?

Exodus 20:5-6
5 You shall not worship them nor serve them; for I, the Lord your God, am a jealous God, inflicting the punishment of the fathers on the children, on the third and the fourth generations of those who hate Me, 6 but showing favor to thousands, to those who love Me and keep My commandments.

Leviticus 26:39
39 So those of you who may be left will rot away because of their wrongdoing in the lands of your enemies; and also because of the wrongdoing of their forefathers they will rot away with them.

Numbers 14:18
18 'The Lord is slow to anger and abundant in mercy, forgiving wrongdoing and violation of His Law; but He will by no means leave the guilty unpunished, inflicting the punishment of the fathers on the children to the third and the fourth generations.'

Remember when I said we have to read all of scripture, even the parts that make us uncomfortable? These are definitely some of those verses. In order to understand these verses, we need to understand that not only is our Heavenly Father loving, but He is also just. If someone came in to your house and did something horrible to your child, would you not seek justice for them? Of course you would, because you love your child. It is not legally just for the guilty to go unpunished, and according to scripture those punishments can and do extend generationally.

Let's look at another scripture passage along these same lines:

> Exodus 34:6-7
> "The Lord, the Lord God, compassionate and gracious, slow to anger, and abounding in lovingkindness and truth; 7 who keeps lovingkindness for thousands, who forgives **iniquity, transgression and sin;** yet He will by no means leave the guilty unpunished, **visiting** the **iniquity** of fathers on the children and on the grandchildren to the third and fourth generations."

The words highlighted in bold are three different Hebrew words for sin. Many times, when we think scripture is just repeating itself, it is actually being specific about something. This verse is showing us that there are different levels of sin. If you study the Hebrew words used here you will see that the word iniquity used means a deep level of sin that effects generations. The Hebrew word for visiting in this scripture is "paqad" which means to punish. In fact, this same Hebrew word is translated to the English word punish over 50 other times in scripture.

Here are some New Testament examples of sin bringing punishment.

Acts 12:22-23
22 The people kept crying out, "The voice of a god and not of a man!" 23 And immediately an angel of the Lord struck him because he did not give God the glory, and he was eaten by worms and died.

John 5:14
14 Afterward Jesus found him in the temple and said to him, "Behold, you have become well; do not sin anymore, so that nothing worse happens to you."

Acts 5:5-11
5 But a man named Ananias, with his wife Sapphira, sold a piece of property, 2 and kept

back some of the price for himself, with his wife's full knowledge, and bringing a portion of it, he laid it at the apostles' feet. 3 But Peter said, "Ananias, why has Satan filled your heart to lie to the Holy Spirit and to keep back some of the price of the land? 4 While it remained unsold, did it not remain your own? And after it was sold, was it not under your control? Why is it that you have conceived this deed in your heart? You have not lied to men but to God." 5 And as he heard these words, Ananias fell down and breathed his last; and great fear came over all who heard of it. 6 The young men got up and covered him up, and after carrying him out, they buried him.

7 Now there elapsed an interval of about three hours, and his wife came in, not knowing what had happened. 8 And Peter responded to her, "Tell me whether you sold the land for such and such a price?" And she said, "Yes, that was the price." 9 Then Peter said to her, "Why is it that you have agreed together to put the Spirit of the Lord to the test? Behold, the feet of those who have buried your husband are at the door, and they will carry you out as well." 10 And immediately she fell at his feet and breathed her last, and the young men came in and found her dead, and they carried her out and buried her beside her husband. 11 And great

fear came over the whole church, and over all who heard of these things.

Revelation 2:19-29

19 'I know your deeds, and your love and faith and service and perseverance, and that your deeds of late are greater than at first. 20 But I have this against you, that you tolerate the woman Jezebel, who calls herself a prophetess, and she teaches and leads My bond-servants astray so that they commit acts of immorality and eat things sacrificed to idols. 21 I gave her time to repent, and she does not want to repent of her immorality. 22 Behold, I will throw her on a bed of sickness, and those who commit adultery with her into great tribulation, unless they repent of her deeds. 23 And I will kill her children with pestilence, and all the churches will know that I am He who searches the minds and hearts; and I will give to each one of you according to your deeds. 24 But I say to you, the rest who are in Thyatira, who do not hold this teaching, who have not known the deep things of Satan, as they call them—I place no other burden on you. 25 Nevertheless what you have, hold fast until I come. 26 He who overcomes, and he who keeps My deeds until the end, to him I will give authority over the nations; 27 and he shall rule them with a rod of iron, as the vessels of the potter are broken to pieces, as I also have received authority

from My Father; 28 and I will give him the morning star. 29 He who has an ear, let him hear what the Spirit says to the churches.'

The wonderful news is that Jesus redeemed us from the curse or punishment of the law. He broke the power that sin and these generational iniquities have over believers, and we can access the sōzō salvation available to us, IF we follow the instructions outlined in scripture to fully receive the Lord's forgiveness, power, and authority over evil.

However, we have to understand that, just because Jesus broke the power of sin on the cross, it doesn't mean that sin doesn't exist, and it doesn't mean that Christians don't ever sin. It just means that if we confess our sins, truly repent, and forgive others in obedience to the Lord's commands, then that sin doesn't have to have the same power over us. Likewise, Jesus' death and resurrection broke the power of generational curses and iniquity, but that doesn't mean that generational curses and iniquity don't exist anymore or that Christians can't suffer from them. It just means that if we confess our sins, truly repent, and forgive others, just as outlined in scripture, those curses don't have to have the same power over us.

1 John 1:8-10

8 If we claim to be without sin, we deceive ourselves and the truth is not in us. 9 If we confess our sins, he is faithful and just and will forgive us our sins and purify us from all **unrighteousness.** 10 If we claim we have not sinned, we make him out to be a liar and his word is not in us.

As you can see above, even after Jesus' death and resurrection, it is still a requirement for us to confess our sins so that the Lord in his faithfulness and justice can forgive our sins and cleanse us from all unrighteousness. What does that word unrighteousness (adikia) mean in the Greek? You guessed it, iniquity. The deep type of sin that passes down and is "punished" generationally.

Now that we've made the case for generational curses, we can use this principle of duality in scripture to make sure that we understand the power of generational blessings! The good seeds of obedience and faith that we sow today can be stored up in Heaven for our future generations. Here is an example of generational blessing in Timothy's life because of the seeds sown by His grandmother and mother.

2 Timothy 1 3-7

3 I thank God, whom I serve with a clear conscience the way my forefathers did, as I constantly remember you in my prayers night and day, 4 longing to see you, even as I recall your tears, so that I may be filled with joy. 5 For I am mindful of the sincere faith within you, which first dwelt in your grandmother Lois and your mother Eunice, and I am sure that it is in you as well. 6 For this reason I remind you to kindle afresh the gift of God which is in you through the laying on of my hands. 7 For God has not given us a spirit of timidity, but of power and love and discipline.

Some people who grow up in a great Christian family with all kinds of generational blessing stored up for them by their ancestors, have a hard time understanding the effects of generational curses. On the same note, some people who come from a dysfunctional family full of evil, have a hard time grasping the idea of generational blessings, but it's important that we understand both exist and we have the choice right now to decide what we are going to store up for our offspring.

Word Curses

Besides curses as punishment of sin there is also another type of cursing that we should be aware of. This is when people use their mouths to curse others or themselves. The following are some scriptures about blessing and cursing from the mouth.

Proverbs 18:21
Death and life are in the power of the tongue,
And those who love it will eat its fruit.

James 3:8-10
8 But no one can tame the tongue; it is a restless evil and full of deadly poison. 9 With it we bless our Lord and Father, and with it we curse men, who have been made in the likeness of God; 10 from the same mouth come both blessing and cursing. My brethren, these things ought not to be this way.

Even in this New Testament scripture from James, we see that when the mouth curses, it is not harmless, but it is described as a deadly poison.

There is however good news that reassures us from the following verse:

Proverbs 26:2 NASB

> Like a sparrow in its flitting, like a swallow in
> its flying, So a curse without cause does not
> alight.

How do we make sure that a curse coming against us does not have a cause? We make sure that we are walking in righteousness. Can we walk in complete righteousness all the time in our own strength? Absolutely not. This is why we need to regularly confess and repent of our sins and ask the Lord to cleanse us from all iniquity. We also need to make sure we are always walking in forgiveness towards other people, including those who are cursing us.

There is other good news that we see in scripture as well. The Lord can take a curse and turn it into a blessing!

> Deuteronomy 23:5 NASB
> Nevertheless, the Lord your God was not willing
> to listen to Balaam, but the Lord your God turned
> the curse into a blessing for you because the Lord
> your God loves you.

We see throughout scripture that something significant happens when we curse people out loud with our words. The whole reason that the lord miraculously caused only a blessing to come out of the mouth of Balaam was because it would have affected the Israelites in a negative way if he was able to go through with the cursing that he had planned to do.

There is a portion of this book dedicated to breaking the power of word curses. I hope you take it seriously, and it causes you to take a step back and examine the words coming out of your own mouth, and the power of death and life in them.

Can a Christian Have Demons?

Sometimes the largest hindrance to someone's deliverance is that they refuse to admit that they need it. If you don't believe that you need deliverance from a demonic spirit, then you are not going to do what it takes to cast it out!

It's actually a great strategy, if you think about it. I mean, if I was a demon and wanted to stay in someone, I would do my best to convince them that they cannot possibly have a demon.

Where is the scripture that states that Christians can have demons? Well, it's right next to the scripture that says they can't have them. In other words, scripture doesn't state plainly either way, but we do have many things in scripture that we can point to that show it is possible.

To anyone who has been around deliverance ministry, it is more than just possible. It is evident. We have watched demons leave Christians over and over again, but I can understand how someone who is new to deliverance would have a hard time with this concept if they haven't seen it with their own eyes yet. Perhaps, they were even taught in a certain denomination where there is no real emphasis on deliverance, that Christians can't have demons.

I grew up in a First Assembly of God, Pentecostal church and I was taught that Christians can't have demons. Meanwhile, I was tormented throughout all of my childhood, because I needed deliverance, and no one ministered it to me. It just wasn't something our church talked about or did. It was no surprise that in my teens, I completely walked away from the Lord. When I finally chose to make Jesus Lord of my life again in my twenties, it was at a typical American mega-church, and no one talked about or did much deliverance there either. It wasn't until a friend at that church approached me about deliverance that I even thought it was a possibility that I needed it.

After this friend saw my story online about all the car accidents I was in and sickness I had dealt with for so many years, she felt the Holy Spirit tell her to chat with me about her testimony of being set free. I respected her, and I was desperate enough to start looking into the subject. As I read about it in scripture, the Holy Spirit revealed to me that I was in bondage and needed to be free. Once my husband and I actually received deliverance and the Lord broke the curses and delivered us of the demonic spirits, I was physically healed, our financial situation completely turned around and so many other things changed in our lives. After this experience, no one could ever convince me that a Christian cannot have demons or curses coming against them, nor could anyone convince me that the miracle of casting out demons has somehow been done away with. Since my experience alone isn't enough, let's dig into some scripture.

One of the biggest misunderstandings about Christians having demons is that they automatically think you are saying that Christians can be "possessed" by demons. That is absolutely not what I believe. In fact, I don't know any deliverance minister who believes that. This misunderstanding comes from an unfortunate translation in the King James Bible where the Greek word "daimonizomai" is translated as demon-possessed and would be better translated as "demonized" or "under the power of a demon." This has caused great confusion over the years.

If you are a Christian, you belong to the Lord, not demons. Can a Christian be possessed by demons? No. Can a Christian be demonized or have demons that have gained a certain level of power in a part of their lives? Yes, absolutely.

Some people believe that when you accept Jesus as your savior all demons automatically leave you. Some people experience deliverance when they first get saved, and I believe that this is how it's supposed to happen along with water baptism and Holy Spirit Baptism but for some reason in most of the American church, this aspect of conversion to Christianity has been overlooked. People are simply ignoring what was a third of Jesus' ministry, and something He clearly said would be a sign of those who believe; casting out demons! If all we had to do to be delivered was pray a simple prayer to follow Jesus, then why are disciples of Jesus told to preach the gospel AND cast out demons. Why wouldn't Jesus have only said to preach the gospel, period?

34

Below are some scriptures to show that, not only can someone who believes in Jesus as their messiah have a demon, but faith in Jesus as their messiah might even be a requirement for someone to receive deliverance.

Matthew 15:21-28

21 Jesus went away from there, and withdrew into the region of Tyre and Sidon. 22 And a Canaanite woman from that region came out and began to cry out, saying, "Have mercy on me, Lord, Son of David; my daughter is severely demon-possessed *(or demonized)*." 23 But He did not answer her with even a word. And His disciples came up and urged Him, saying, "Send her away, because she keeps shouting at us!" 24 But He answered and said, "I was sent only to the lost sheep of the house of Israel." 25 But she came and began to bow down before Him, saying, "Lord, help me!" 26 Yet He answered and said, "It is not good to take the children's bread and throw it to the dogs." 27 And she said, "Yes, Lord; but please help, for even the dogs feed on the crumbs that fall from their masters' table." 28 Then Jesus said to her, "O woman, your faith is great; it shall be done for you as you desire." And her daughter was healed at once.

As you can see above, this gentile woman was refused deliverance for her daughter by Jesus until after she called Him Lord and Master several times. He told her deliverance was for the "children" meaning "children of God" (who were the Jews at this time.) However, her great faith in Him as the messiah, made Him decide to cast the demon out of her daughter.

Luke 13:10-17

10 Now Jesus was teaching in one of the synagogues on the Sabbath. 11 And there was a woman who for eighteen years had had a sickness caused by a spirit; and she was bent over double, and could not straighten up at all. 12 When Jesus saw her, He called her over and said to her, "Woman, you are freed from your sickness." 13 And He laid His hands on her; and immediately she stood up straight again, and began glorifying God. 14 But the synagogue leader, indignant because Jesus had healed on the Sabbath, began saying to the crowd in response, "There are six days during which work should be done; so come during them and get healed, and not on the Sabbath day." 15 But the Lord answered him and said, "You hypocrites, does each of you on the Sabbath not untie his ox or donkey from the stall and lead it away to water it? 16 And this woman, a daughter of Abraham as she is, whom Satan has bound

for eighteen long years, should she not have been released from this restraint on the Sabbath day?" 17 And as He said this, all His opponents were being humiliated; and the entire crowd was rejoicing over all the glorious things being done by Him.

We see in the scripture above, that the woman who had a demonic spirit of infirmity was referred to by Jesus as a "daughter of Abraham." Galatians 3:6-7 says that those who are justified by faith are sons of Abraham. Now before you think that this was just a term for all Jewish people, remember that when the Jewish leaders told Jesus that they were sons of Abraham, He corrected them and said they were sons of the devil. (John 8:44)

> Matthew 12:43-45
> 43 "Now when the unclean spirit comes out of a person, it passes through waterless places seeking rest, and does not find it. 44 Then it says, 'I will return to my house from which I came'; and when it comes, it finds it unoccupied, swept, and put in order. 45 Then it goes and brings along with it seven other spirits more wicked than itself, and they come in and live there; and the last condition of that person becomes worse than the first. That is the way it will also be with this evil generation."

It is the passage above that makes me leery of doing deliverance on anyone who isn't a true follower of Jesus Christ and hasn't received the Holy Spirit. I do not want to just cast a spirit out of someone who doesn't carry any spiritual authority in Christ, only to have it come back with its friends and then that person is worse off than before. Also, many times as demons are being cast out they will resist and say something like "she is mine!" We can only stand against that as a lie, when the person is truly the Lord's.

Spiritual Warfare

Some people are very hesitant to engage in spiritual warfare. This was me for a long time. The enemy had me pinned down in fear, that if I would exercise my authority in Jesus Christ and cast out demons, I would be putting myself in danger. Actually, the opposite was true. When you become a believer in Jesus' Christ and start living for Him, you are already in a war and the enemy is going to attack you whether you engage in battle or not. The question is: Are you an easy target? Do you just allow the enemy to torment you with his evil spirits, or do you stand in your authority in Jesus Christ and cast them out like we are told to do in scripture?

On the flip side, there are many people who start waging war against things in the spirit that the Lord never told them to do. These are the people who are going around addressing all the principalities over regions and binding Satan and such. This is also not recommended. Many times, these people will come under attacks that are unnecessary to their calling, because they are antagonizing the enemy by addressing him in their own flesh.

Scripture says that Satan will not be bound until it is his time, and you are not the angel who will bind Him. On this same note, I do not recommend that you address Satan directly, in general. For wisdom on how to do warfare with the enemy, we can look to Jesus. Jesus did not go around binding every principality and trying to talk to Satan. Even when Satan approached Jesus to tempt Him in the wilderness, Jesus replied to him with scripture and just told him to go away. When Satan used Peter to try to convince Jesus not to go to the cross, He simply said, "Get behind Me, Satan! You are a stumbling block to Me; for you are not setting your mind on God's purposes, but men's." (Matthew 16:23)

Matthew 4:1-11

Then Jesus was led up by the Spirit into the wilderness to be tempted by the devil. 2 And after He had fasted for forty days and forty nights, He then became hungry. 3 And the tempter came and said to Him, "If You are the Son of God, command that these stones become bread." 4 But He answered and said, "It is written: 'Man shall not live on bread alone, but on every word that comes out of the mouth of God.'"

5 Then the devil took Him along into the holy city and had Him stand on the pinnacle of the temple, 6 and he said to Him, "If You are the Son of God, throw Yourself down; for it is written:

'He will give His angels orders concerning You'; And 'On their hands they will lift You up, So that You do not strike Your foot against a stone.'"

7 Jesus said to him, "On the other hand, it is written: 'You shall not put the Lord your God to the test.'"

8 Again, the devil took Him along to a very high mountain and showed Him all the kingdoms of the world and their glory; 9 and he said to Him, "All these things I will give You, if You fall down and worship me." 10 Then Jesus *said to him, "Go away, Satan! For it is written: 'You shall worship the Lord your God, and serve Him only.'" 11 Then the devil left Him; and behold, angels came and began to serve Him.

The Deliverance Ministry of Jesus

I recommend taking the time to look up each of these scriptures to study the deliverance ministry of Jesus and what it looked like when he casted out demons.

Many people delivered
Mark 1:32-34, Matthew 8:16-17, Luke 4:40-41, Mark 1:39, Matthew 4:24, Luke 7:21, Luke 6:17-19, Mark 3:10-12

A man at the Capernaum Synagogue
Mark 1:21-28, Luke 4:31-37

Men in Capernaum who could speak once the demons were cast out
Matthew 9:32-33, Matthew 12:22, Luke 11:14

The Gentile woman's daughter
Matthew 15:21-28, Mark 7:24-30

Mary Magdalene (and many other women who supported Jesus' ministry)
Luke 8:2, Mark 16:9

The Gadarene men at the tombs
Matthew 8:28-32, Mark 5:1-13, Luke 8:26-33

<u>A man's son at Caesarea Philippi that the disciples</u>
<u>couldn't cast out but Jesus did</u>
Matthew 16:13, Matthew 17:14-21, Mark 9:17-29,
Luke 9:38-47

<u>The woman who Jesus called a "daughter of</u>
<u>Abraham" who had a spirit of infirmity for 18</u>
<u>years</u>
Luke 13:10-17

<u>Jesus accused by religious people of having a</u>
<u>demon and casting out demons by the power of</u>
<u>Satan</u>
Luke 11:15-26, Mark 3:22-30, John 8:39-52, John
10:19-21

<u>The Pharisees try to get Jesus to leave, but he tells</u>
<u>them he hasn't reached his goal of casting out</u>
<u>demons and doing healings yet.</u>
Luke 13:31-32

Deliverance Ministry of Believers

We see in scripture that not only did Jesus cast
out demons but He also trained His followers to
do it as well. Then, He even went on to say that a
sign of anyone who believes is that they will cast
out demons.

Instruction from Jesus to heal the sick, raise the dead, cleanse those with leprosy, cast out demons freely.
Matthew 10:5-8

Jesus gives the disciples authority over unclean spirits
Matthew 10:1, Mark 3:14-15, Mark 6:7

Casting out demons as evidence of those who believe
Mark 16:17-18,

The 72 disciples sent out came back excited that the demons were subject to them in Jesus' name.
Luke 10:17-20

Jesus says to let the others who are casting out demons keep doing it even though they weren't part of their group.
Mark 9:38-40, Luke 9:49-50

Believers casting out many demons and healing people
Mark 6:13, Acts 8:6-8

Paul gets annoyed at a spirit of divination and casts it out of a woman

Acts 16:18

<u>The Lord uses handkerchiefs and aprons from
Paul to cast out demons and heal people</u>
Acts 19:11-12

Do you Have Power and Authority in Christ?

It is not recommended that anyone who is not a believer and true follower of Jesus Christ of Nazareth, pray any of the deliverance prayers in this book or try to cast out demons. It is only those who are born again as His followers that carry the power and authority in Christ to cast out demons.

Unfortunately, someone who does not carry the authority in Christ and tries to do deliverance could run into quite a bit of trouble. You can read about the sons of Sceva (Acts 19:11-20).

Today, it is very common for people to assume that if they once prayed a little prayer to "ask Jesus into their heart", that they are automatically saved. However, there is no such thing in scripture.

We are truly saved by Jesus Christ when our old self is crucified with Christ and we are born again into the kingdom of God. This means that salvation doesn't come when we just ask Jesus to be a part of our life. It comes when we believe in Him enough that we give him our ENTIRE life. This means that you are choosing to follow His commands and repent of (or turn away from) all known sin and obey Him instead.

Jesus is not just our Savior and Friend. He must be our Lord. This means that we do not just call Him Lord, but actually do the will of His Father in Heaven; who becomes our Father in Heaven when we are reborn. When I read the scriptures, I've noticed that Jesus, did not go around casting demons out of unbelievers. He didn't go around casting demons out of the Pharisees, even though they were so full of them that He called them a brood of vipers. The pagan girl recorded in scripture that received deliverance from Jesus was the daughter of the Canaanite woman whom Jesus refused at first. After she called Him master and Lord, confessing her faith in Him as the Messiah multiple times, He decided to deliver her daughter. Even the Gadarene man at the tombs that Jesus freed from a legion of demons came and fell on His knees before Jesus. (Mark 5:6) I believe this sign of the man's surrender to Jesus, was what caused the demon to manifest and start talking. I cannot say that Jesus never did deliverance on a non-believer, but I do know from the examples that we have, that over and over again, people showed their faith in Him before receiving miracles of deliverance and healing.

Here are some scriptures about giving our lives to Christ and being born again.

Galatians 2:20
I have been crucified with Christ; and it is no longer I who live, but Christ lives in me; and the life which I now live in the flesh I live by faith in the Son of God, who loved me and gave Himself up for me.

2 Corinthians 5:17
Therefore, if anyone is in Christ, this person is a new creation; the old things passed away; behold, new things have come.

Matthew 7:21
"Not everyone who says to me, 'Lord, Lord,' will enter the kingdom of heaven, but only the one who does the will of my Father who is in heaven.

Acts 2:38

Peter said to them, "Repent, and each of you be baptized in the name of Jesus Christ for the forgiveness of your sins; and you will receive the gift of the Holy Spirit.

Titus 3:5

he saved us, not because of righteous things we had done, but because of his mercy. He saved us through the washing of rebirth and renewal by the Holy Spirit.

John 3:16-18

"For God so loved the world, that He gave His only Son, so that everyone who believes in Him will not perish, but have eternal life. For God did not send the Son into the world to judge the world, but so that the world might be saved through Him. The one who believes in Him is not judged; the one who does not believe has been judged already, because he has not believed in the name of the only Son of God.

Opening Prayers

Prayer of Salvation in Jesus Christ

Remember this prayer is not a formula to follow to get into Heaven. If you are not truly repentant and if you do not believe, in faith, everything that you pray, it will not do anything, but make you believe that you are saved; when you're not. That is a dangerous place to be. If you are truly ready and desperate for the Lord to save you; If you are ready to give Him EVERYTHING; Then you will not just read this prayer, but actually pray this prayer from your heart.

Prayer of Faith

Lord Jesus Christ of Nazareth, I believe that you came to this earth and died for me. I believe that you were resurrected on the third day. I choose today to turn from all sin; everything in my life that goes against my Creator, Adonai, and His will for my life as outlined in Holy Scripture. I confess that Jesus Christ (Yeshua Hamashiach) is Lord of my life. He is my savior and redeemer. By grace, through my faith in Him, I am now a child of God. My Creator, Adonai, is now my Heavenly Father. I give you my whole life Lord, not my will, but yours be done.

Father, Jesus Christ, and Holy Spirit, I give back to you all that I am; my spiritual gifts, my strengths & weaknesses, my failures and successes, my personality and my abilities. Please purify, cleanse and refine them. They belong to you. I only want what you have designed and chosen for me and I want to bring you glory with all that I am, and all you have created me to be.

I believe that it is your will that I walk in freedom and divine health. Jesus, I ask you today to cleanse me and heal me; Spirit, Soul, and Body. Lord, I welcome you into every part of my being. Baptize me and fill me with Your Holy Spirit that gives me power to be a witness for Jesus Christ. Speak to me and guide me, show me how to pray. Help me live according to your divine purpose for my life. I ask this in the mighty name of Jesus, Amen

Taking Authority

Besides the true and full gospel of salvation in Jesus Christ, another thing that is important to understand is your authority in Christ. This is also received by faith and that faith is evident by our love and obedience to the Lord. Many times, when doing deliverance, a spirit will try to convince you that they have the right to be in your life or that you don't have the authority to tell them to go, but you must be firm in your faith. Insist that it leave you immediately. Do not back down. Obviously, if the Lord shows you that there is an open door that you need to close, or a legal right that you need to break, go ahead, and do that, but that should be under guidance and revelation from the Lord, not a demon.

Self-deliverance can be done, and has been done by people who are walking in the authority of Jesus, but ideally you will have a mature, Holy Spirit filled believer to pray these prayers with you. It's helpful to have another person who is standing in agreement with you, listening to the Lord with you, and ministering deliverance to you when needed. A person ministering deliverance to another person is what we most commonly see in scripture.

James 5:16 tells us to confess our sins to each other and pray for each other, so that we can be healed. This word for healed is the Greek word "iaomai," which means to cure, heal, make whole, save from sins, and bring about one's salvation. Ask the Lord for guidance in this area. There may be some things that He allows you to pray about on your own, and some that He tells you to have another person minister to you.

The most important thing, is that you are led by the Holy Spirit in obedience to the Lord and His plan for your deliverance. Only He knows everything that you are dealing with and how He wants to go about freeing you. It will be the way that brings Him the most glory, and is most beneficial to you. I believe the Holy Spirit will reveal direction as you ask and wait on Him. Remember, the Lord isn't just interested in you being free from bondage for a moment of relief. He wants you to be completely free and stay free; living a life of victory and purpose in Him!

Hindrances to Deliverance

The following are some hindrances to deliverance as well as prayers of freedom to break them off of your life.

Fear

Some people are afraid of deliverance ministry because they see scriptures like what happened to the sons of Sceba, but it's important to note that those men were not true followers of our Messiah, Jesus. If you know Jesus and walk in obedience to Him, you will have authority over demons. Some become fearful, because of their interpretation of Matthew 12:43-45 where the spirit came back to its home with 7 other spirits more wicked than itself.

This scripture has been interpreted so many different ways over the years. I'm not sure anyone has it perfectly right, but there are some key things that I see in it that I believe are reassuring. First, the scripture does not say that this spirit was "cast out" of the person. Most translations say when a spirit "goes out" or "comes out." I don't necessarily believe that this passage has to do with someone who went through actual deliverance, but possibly someone who a demon has gone out of for a time. This could be someone who has tried to clean up their act on their own and did it so well that the demon decided to leave for a time, but its's apparent that this demon still had the right to come back if it wanted to.

Also, notice how the house was swept clean and empty. If you are filled with the Holy Spirit, you are not empty. Thirdly, the spirit calls the person it's home. If you are repentant and demons are cast out of you, then you are no longer that demon's home. It's also important to make sure that when you get delivered, you close the door on that demon that might seek to come back by living a lifestyle of repentance and obedience to the Father.

I am also comforted by the following verse, which promises authority and protection when dealing with evil spirits. To understand this verse, you need to read it with the Hebraic mindset that it was written. You must understand that all throughout scripture, snakes and scorpions represent evil spirits.

> Luke 10:19
> Behold, I have given you authority to tread on serpents and scorpions, and over all the power of the enemy, and nothing will injure you.

Prayer of Freedom

Dear Heavenly Father, You have not given me a spirit of fear, but of power, love and a sound mind. I confess on behalf of myself and my ancestors that we have allowed fear and anxiety to exercise control over our lives, instead of trusting in You. I ask you to forgive us and break the power of any curse it may have caused. I now confess, renounce and reject all ungodly fear and anxiety. I confess that the Lord has given me authority over evil spirits and all the power of the enemy. He protects me as I minister deliverance to myself and others.

In Jesus' name, I command every spirit of fear, anxiety, and doubt to leave me now. Lord, I pray that You would fill me with Your Holy Spirit, that I may live a life without fear and I may speak your Word and move in Your power and authority with boldness. In Jesus' name, I pray. Amen.

Pause and ask the Lord if there is anything else He would like you to pray or declare, and continue as the Holy Spirit leads you.

Pride and Rebellion

We have to want to be free more than we care about looking good, and we have to want to be free more than we want to do our own will. In my experience with deliverance ministry, I've noticed that people who are ready to humble themselves before God and before man, openly confess their sins, and repent, are usually the ones that get free the fastest. Stubbornness, pride, and ego definitely slow down or even halt the process.

Prayer of Freedom

Dear Heavenly Father, Your word says that pride goes before destruction and a haughty spirit before a fall. (Prov. 16:18) and rebellion is the sin of witchcraft (1 Samuel 15:23).

I confess that I have lived independently of You, giving ground to the enemy in my life. I have believed that I could be successful and live victoriously by my own strength and resources. I now confess that my ancestors and I have sinned against You by placing our will before Yours and by centering our lives around self instead of You. I confess that we have not obeyed You. We have rebelled in our hearts against You, and against those You have placed in authority over us.

I ask you Father to forgive me and my ancestors for the sins of pride and rebellion. I pray that all ground gained by evil spirits in my life due to these sins would be cancelled. Holy Spirit, close and seal all doors that may have been opened to me and my offspring. Seal them with the blood of the Lord Jesus Christ of Nazareth. I choose now to submit to the Lord and Godly authority that

He has placed in my life. Father, I ask that you would give me a servant's heart.

I renounce and reject the idol of self, and cancel all the ground that has been gained in my family by the kingdom of darkness. I pray that You will fill me, Holy Spirit, and guide me so that I will do nothing from selfishness or empty conceit, but with humility of mind, I will regard others as more important than myself (Phil. 2:3). Help me to remain humble and always choose your will above my own; no matter what that might look like.
I pray this in the mighty name of Jesus, Amen.

Pause and ask the Lord if there is anything else He would like you to pray or declare, and continue as the Holy Spirit leads you.

Insincere Repentance

We may be able to act sincere and read a prayer from this book to put on a show for other people, but we cannot fool the Lord Most High. He knows if you are truly repentant with your whole heart, or if you are just looking for some quick relief, so that you can just go back to living in rebellion; opening the door back up to the enemy.

We can easily get frustrated when the deliverance that we are believing for doesn't happen right away. Sometimes, it's the Lord's mercy for Him to wait for the right time, when we are finally in the right place to truly turn from sin.

Prayer of Freedom

Father God, I ask you today to help me to truly repent of everything in my life that doesn't honor you. Give me the courage, strength, and conviction to get rid of anything I own that dishonors you in any way. Show me the areas of my life that I have not fully surrendered to you, and help me live a life of full obedience and righteousness in your sight. In Jesus' name, Amen.

Pause and ask the Lord if there is anything else He would like you to pray or declare, and continue as the Holy Spirit leads you.

Doubt and Unbelief

Faith is required to see signs, wonders and miracles. Deliverance is a miracle of the Lord. Even Jesus himself was hindered from doing miracles in His own hometown where people were too familiar with Him, and didn't believe in His power (Mark 6:5).

I've found this in deliverance ministry as well. People tend to be delivered much faster when they aren't too familiar with the person ministering to them. Power flows much more freely when we believe in the Lord's power to heal, and when we believe in the authority that we or the person ministering to us carries in Christ. Jesus would often ask people if they believed that He could heal them, before He did so. I believe the simple "Yes," from those people, was an act of faith in Him and His power to do wonders.

Prayer of Freedom

Heavenly Father, I confess on behalf of myself and my ancestors for partnering with doubt and unbelief. I ask you to forgive us for hindering your power from flowing through us and others. I command all spirits associated with doubt and unbelief to leave me and my family now in Jesus' name. Father, I ask you to break every curse of doubt and unbelief that has come down to me generationally. Cleanse my bloodline of all unrighteousness in this area. I declare that I am full of faith and trust in You and Your plan for my deliverance. Show me where I have become too familiar with people, and have doubted that You could move mightily through them. Help me truly understand the authority that I carry in your name, Jesus. May I exercise that authority boldly, and without fear or doubt. It is not by our own might or power, but by Your Spirit that we perform signs, wonders, and miracles. It is not by our own righteousness that we qualify ourselves, but by grace, through faith in Jesus did for us.

Pause and ask the Lord if there is anything else He would like you to pray or declare, and continue as the Holy Spirit leads you.

Unforgiveness

Scripture says unforgiveness can be a hindrance to the Lord forgiving you (Matthew 6:15). If it can hinder the Lord from forgiving you, then it can surely hinder deliverance, since the Lord's forgiveness is a requirement for our freedom.

Forgiveness is not forgetting. Forgetting may be the result of forgiveness, but it is never the means of forgiveness. Forgiveness is cancelling any revenge that we would seek out towards a person and giving that to God to deal with as He wills.

Forgiveness doesn't make what this person did okay. It just releases you from the enemy having an open door to you because of your bitterness.

Forgiveness is a choice. It is something we can do, but it can be difficult. This is where we can ask the Holy Spirit to help us. Your need to forgive is not an issue between you and the offender, it is between you and God.

To forgive is to acknowledge the offense and how it hurt you, let the Lord heal your soul of the wounds that were caused, and decide that you will not use this person's actions against them in the future. This doesn't mean that you must tolerate sin or abuse, and this doesn't mean that you stay in a dangerous situation with someone who is still hurting you. Boundaries can be healthy and necessary.

Choose to forgive quickly. If you wait to forgive until you feel like it: you will never do it. Feelings take time to heal after the choice to forgive is made, but Satan has lost his place (Eph. 4:26-27) Freedom is what will be gained right away, not a feeling. Allow the Holy Spirit to reveal to you anyone in your life that you may still need to forgive.

Prayer of Freedom

Dear Heavenly Father, I thank you that your kindness has led me to repentance (Romans 2:4). I confess that I have struggled to extend that same patience and kindness toward others who have offended me. I confess that I have harbored bitterness and resentment. I pray that during this time of self-examination, You would bring to my mind those people that I have not forgiven, so that I may begin the process of forgiveness (Matt.18:35). Lord I ask you to also show me those whom I have hurt or offended, so that I can ask for their forgiveness.

Lord, I choose to forgive __name all offender(s)__.

I forgive them for __(specifically identify all offences) _.

It made me feel _____, and Lord, I give you that wound, and ask You to heal me.

I release all these people to You Lord, and my right to seek revenge. I choose not to hold onto my bitterness and anger, and I ask You to heal every wound in my soul that these offences have caused.

Lord, forgive me for my unforgiveness. I know that my struggle is not against flesh and blood, but the enemy has used these people and their hurting souls to cause me pain. I claim back everything the enemy has stolen from me and my family through this battle. I give all the pain of betrayal, and all the suspicion and mistrust that I've been carrying to you, Father. I renounce every evil thought of revenge and I give these people and all these situations to you Lord. Only you know how to deal with them justly. I command all spirits of bitterness and unforgiveness to leave me now in Jesus' name. I declare that my life is full of joy and shalom peace from the Lord almighty. He has healed the wounds in my soul, delivered me, and made me whole.

I pray Father God, that you would heal, deliver, and bless these people. I pray that they would become closer to You than they ever have been. I pray that they would walk in obedience to You and that Your perfect will be done in their lives.

Pause and ask the Lord if there is anything else He would like you to pray or declare, and continue as the Holy Spirit leads you.

The participant may benefit from parental affirmation or apology on behalf of the authority figure that hurt them (pastor, parent etc.)

General Prayer to Break Off Hindrances

Heavenly Father, thank You that your will is for me to be free. Thank you that you have sent your Son to die for me and be resurrected that I might have freedom and eternal life. I recognize You have a plan for me and I submit myself to that plan. I choose to set aside any distractions, pride, or resistance to You. I surrender my life to You, Father God, to Your Holy Spirit and to Your Son Jesus Christ. I give You all of the glory and praise for what you have already done in my life and are about to do.

I repent of any actions or words on my part that have hindered You in any way from fulfilling whatever You want to do in my life. I confess on behalf of myself and my ancestors that we have walked in fear, pride, rebellion, doubt, unforgiveness, and ___anything else the Holy Spirit reveals___.

I ask you Father to forgive us. I renounce and turn from all lies, preconceptions, deceptions, and unteachableness that I or my ancestors have believed or entertained. I ask to be cleansed from them by the blood of the Lord Jesus Christ.

I come out of agreement with and renounce all shame, blame, guilt, and fear. This includes all fear of failure, fear of rejection, fear of man, fear of evil, and all fear of not hearing the Lord.

Holy Spirit I ask that you would fill me, baptize me in your power. I ask that you would give me words of knowledge and discernment of spirits. Thank you for giving me the boldness and courage to exercise the power and authority that I have in Jesus Christ to cast out all evil from my life and the lives of others.

In the name of Jesus, I break and I sever all pride and rebellion. I break their hold on my life. I choose to follow You, Adonai, and receive all that you want to give me in this moment.

I renounce all vows of secrecy and silence about all ungodly activities.

I bind every evil spirit that is trying to hinder my deliverance in Jesus Christ. You no longer have any power to keep me in bondage. In the name of Jesus, I command you to leave me now, and never return to me or anyone I love.

I command that every evil spirit trying to hinder me from the fullness of my calling in Christ Jesus leave me today, I forbid you to become violent or cause any negative symptoms as you leave.

Thank you, Lord, for complete protection from all evil for everyone in my deliverance. In Jesus' name I pray.

Pause and ask the Lord if there is anything else He would like you to pray or declare, and continue as the Holy Spirit leads you.

Hearing the Voice of God

Deliverance and healing is not a religious program or standard formula. It is imperative that you are able to listen to the voice of the Lord through the whole process. He is the one who will reveal the things which are hidden.

It is not recommended that you go and dig up everything from your past, or repeatedly pray these prayers confessing sins that you've already confessed and repenting of things you've already been freed from. This is one way the enemy can trap you in religion and unbelief. If the enemy can convince you that you aren't free when you are, it opens the door for him to come back into your life again.

Likewise, there are many things that people don't realize that they still need freedom from. One of the greatest deceptions of the enemy is to convince someone who really does need freedom from something, that they don't have any bondage. He will convince them that they don't need to confess their sin out loud, or renounce all evil they or their ancestors have given place to. This keeps people from actually doing what it takes to cast out demons.

Remember, when you are dealing with a demon, it will do everything it can to convince you that you are free, when you are not, because it does not want to be seen, acknowledged, and kicked out of your life. It knows that if you don't believe it is there, you will not cast it out.

It's also important to remember that when you are free, that spirit will eventually try to convince you of the lie that you are not free, so that it has a way back in through you believing that lie.

The only way that we can overcome this is by revelation of the Holy Spirit. Don't rely on the enemy or your own mind to tell you what is going on. Let the Lord tell you what needs to be dealt with. The Lord promises us in His word, that if we will diligently and earnestly seek Him, and wait on Him with our whole heart, He will reveal things to us that we otherwise would not have known.

Scriptures About Hearing God

Jeremiah 33:3 ESV - Call to me and I will answer you, and will tell you great and hidden things that you have not known.

Proverbs 3:5-6 ESV - Trust in the Lord with all your heart, and do not lean on your own understanding. In all your ways acknowledge him, and he will make straight your paths.

Psalm 25:4-5 ESV - Make me to know your ways, O Lord; teach me your paths. Lead me in your truth and teach me, for you are the God of my salvation; for you I wait all the day long.

Psalm 37:4-5 ESV - Delight yourself in the Lord, and he will give you the desires of your heart. Commit your way to the Lord; trust in him, and he will act.

Jeremiah 29:11-13 - For I know the plans that I have for you,' declares the Lord, 'plans for prosperity and not for disaster, to give you a future and a hope. Then you will call upon Me and come and pray to Me, and I will listen to you. And you will seek Me and find Me when you search for Me with all your heart.

Proverbs 2:1-5 ESV - My son, if you receive my words and treasure up my commandments with you, making your ear attentive to wisdom and inclining your heart to understanding; yes, if you call out for insight and raise your voice for understanding, if you seek it like silver and search for it as for hidden treasures, then you will understand the fear of the Lord and find the knowledge of God.

Psalm 37:7-9 ESV - Be still before the Lord and wait patiently for him; fret not yourself over the one who prospers in his way, over the man who carries out evil devices! Refrain from anger, and forsake wrath! Fret not yourself; it tends only to evil. For the evildoers shall be cut off, but those who wait for the Lord shall inherit the land.

1 Corinthians 2:14 ESV - The natural person does not accept the things of the Spirit of God, for they are folly to him, and he is not able to understand them because they are spiritually discerned.

Deuteronomy 28:1-2 ESV - And if you faithfully obey the voice of the Lord your God, being careful to do all his commandments that I command you today, the Lord your God will set you high above all the nations of the earth. And all these blessings shall come upon you and overtake you, if you obey the voice of the Lord your God.

Matthew 6:33 ESV - But seek first the kingdom of God and his righteousness, and all these things will be added to you.

Hebrews 3:15 ESV - As it is said, "Today, if you hear his voice, do not harden your hearts as in the rebellion."

John 16:13 ESV - When the Spirit of truth comes, he will guide you into all the truth, for he will not speak on his own authority, but whatever he hears he will speak, and he will declare to you the things that are to come.

John 5:30 ESV - "I can do nothing on my own. As I hear, I judge, and my judgment is just, because I seek not my own will but the will of him who sent me.

Deuteronomy 13:4 ESV - You shall walk after the Lord your God and fear him and keep his commandments and obey his voice, and you shall serve him and hold fast to him.

Matthew 7:24 ESV - "Everyone then who hears these words of mine and does them will be like a wise man who built his house on the rock.

Hebrews 12:25 ESV - See that you do not refuse him who is speaking. For if they did not escape when they refused him who warned them on earth, much less will we escape if we reject him who warns from heaven.

Mark 4:18-19 ESV - And others are the ones sown among thorns. They are those who hear the word, but the cares of the world and the deceitfulness of riches and the desires for other things enter in and choke the word, and it proves unfruitful.

Proverbs 1:20-33 ESV - 20 Wisdom shouts in the street, She raises her voice in the public square; 21 At the head of the noisy streets she cries out; At the entrance of the gates in the city she declares her sayings: 22 "How long, you naive ones, will you love simplistic thinking? And how long will scoffers delight themselves in scoffing and fools hate knowledge? 23 Turn to my rebuke, Behold, I will pour out my spirit on you; I will make my words known to you. 24 Because I called and you refused, I stretched out my hand and no one paid attention; 25 And you neglected all my advice and did not want my rebuke; 26 I will also laugh at your disaster; I will mock when your dread comes, 27 When your dread comes like a storm and your disaster comes like a whirlwind, when distress and anguish come upon you. 28 Then they will call on me, but I will not answer; They will seek me diligently but will not find me, 29 Because they hated knowledge and did not choose the fear of the Lord. 30 They did not accept my advice. They disdainfully rejected every rebuke from me. 31 So they shall eat of the fruit of their own way, and be filled with their own schemes. 32 For the faithlessness of the naive will kill them, And the complacency of fools will destroy them. 33 But whoever listens to me will live securely and will be at ease from the dread of evil.

Removing Hindrances to Hearing God

Sometimes we miss out on things that the Lord has for us, because we do not diligently seek Him enough. In our culture today, people want the easy button, but God is not our genie in a bottle. He is the Holy and Righteous One, The Sovereign Most High God. He does not have to tell us anything. However, in His goodness and mercy, He promises that if we seek him and wait on him with all our heart, we will find Him. He speaks to us and guides us, because He loves us.

Sometimes, the Lord may test us, to see how serious we really are. Are we just looking for quick relief so that we can go back to our old selfish habits? or are we willing to fully submit to Him and His will for our lives? What will we do with the freedom He gives us? Our own will? Or His?

If you aren't Hearing the Lord right away, do not give up. Press in harder, in prayer and fasting. If hearing from the Lord has always been a bit of a struggle, or you feel there is something blocking you from truly listening to his voice. Then there might be something there to pray about. Has there been a time where you chose not to hear the

Lord, because you didn't want the responsibility of doing what He said? Have you ever filtered what the Lord has spoken to you through an idol that you placed before Him in your life? Have you or your ancestors ever disobeyed the word of the Lord that was written or spoken?

Matthew 13:10-17
And the disciples came up and said to Him, "Why do You speak to them in parables?" And Jesus answered them, "To you it has been granted to know the mysteries of the kingdom of heaven, but to them it has not been granted. For whoever has, to him more shall be given, and he will have an abundance; but whoever does not have, even what he has shall be taken away from him. Therefore, I speak to them in parables; because while seeing they do not see, and while hearing they do not hear, nor do they understand. And in their case the prophecy of Isaiah is being fulfilled, which says,

'You shall keep on listening, but shall not understand; and you shall keep on looking, but shall not perceive;
For the heart of this people has become dull,
With their ears they scarcely hear,
And they have closed their eyes,
Otherwise, they might see with their eyes,
Hear with their ears,

Understand with their heart, and return,
And I would heal them.'

But blessed are your eyes, because they see; and your ears, because they hear. For truly I say to you that many prophets and righteous people longed to see what you see, and did not see it, and to hear what you hear, and did not hear it.

Isaiah 59:1-2
Behold, the Lord's hand is not shortened, that it cannot save; nor His ear heavy, that it cannot hear. But your iniquities have separated you from your God and your sins have hidden His face from you, so that He will not hear.

Psalm 66:17-20 ESV
Come and hear, all you who fear God,
    and I will tell what he has done for my soul.
I cried to him with my mouth,
    and high praise was on my tongue.
If I had cherished iniquity in my heart,
    the Lord would not have listened.
But truly God has listened;
    he has attended to the voice of my prayer.
Blessed be God, because he has not rejected my prayer or removed his steadfast love from me!

Prayer of Freedom

Heavenly Father, I confess the sin of my ancestors and my own sin of being unwilling to hear, see and understand the things that You chose to share with us, and for not acting in faith on what we did hear, see or understand. Forgive us Lord, for choosing to be insensitive, hard-hearted, and calloused to Your Word, written (Logos) or spoken (Rhema).

You showed us, but we chose not to see. You spoke to us, but we chose not to hear. We failed to take the time to seek you and understand what You were saying to us. I confess, that we have put idols before you and the words You've spoken to us.

I forgive my ancestors for these sins, and for the consequences that have come down to my family and me. I forgive myself for falling into this same sin. I ask you, Lord, to forgive my ancestors and me for these sins that have hindered our ability to hear you clearly. I ask you Father, in Jesus' name, to break every curse and cleanse my bloodline from all iniquity.

In the mighty name of Jesus Christ, I renounce all evil that has given power to this rebellion. I break all evil generational ties from the beginning of time to the current generation. Every evil spirit that is hindering me from fully hearing and understanding the Lord's voice, I command you to leave me now in the name of Jesus Christ my King.

Heavenly Father, I choose to hear, to see and to understand what You say to me, so that I can apply it to my life and do everything You have called me to do. Bless my eyes to see and my ears to hear. May I see the things that you show me to do. May I use the knowledge that you've given to me, so that I will be given more. Just like you promise in your word.

Give me faith to believe for what You show me. Give me a bold confidence and peace to believe without any doubt that I have heard you correctly. Lord, sharpen my vision, my hearing, and my focus. Help me to know your perfect strategy, in every situation. I pray this in Jesus' name. Amen!

Pause and ask the Lord if there is anything else He would like you to pray or declare, and continue as the Holy Spirit leads you.

Renouncement Prayers by Topic

The following is a collection of several prayers organized by topic. Ask the Holy Spirit to reveal to you which topics to pray about. Remember, these prayers are not a religious formula. What is important is that you are truly repentant and praying from your heart, in faith, by the authority of Christ. These prayers are just a helpful tool to help you find the words to say and what could be related to that topic that you might want to address.

Always, always, pause, and ask the Lord if there is more that He wants you to pray, or if there is anything else He wants to reveal to you.

I've included some example lists of things to renounce throughout this book. Some of these lists seem long, but they are included to help people see what could have been an open door to the enemy in their life. Often, when I am ministering deliverance to someone, the Lord will reveal to me that they need to repent of something, like witchcraft, that they or their ancestors have participated in. Many times, they will quickly deny ever being involved in such a thing. I will explain to them that it could possibly be just in their generational line and suggest that we look through the list, and ask the Lord to reveal what it could have been. Often, when we look at the list together, they end up letting me know of about a dozen things on there that they have actually done themselves. They either totally forgot until they saw it on paper, or they didn't realize that it was an act of witchcraft when they did it. This is one reason why these lists are included in the book.

Some people might choose to prayerfully look over the lists before the prayers, and highlight the things the Lord reveals to them. Many will just confess everything on the list, just in case it's been in their family somewhere along the line. When you think about what could come down generationally, there's a lot of people involved that you might not even know personally. You have 2 parents, 4 grandparents, 8 great grandparents, 16 great-great grandparents and so on. That's a lot of opportunity for sin to creep in and go unconfessed. However you choose to work through these lists, is up to you and God. They are just here to assist you as you listen to the voice of the Lord on what to do. He might highlight something on a list to you. He might speak a word to you when you pause that isn't even on the list. You might not even know what that word means. Trust Him and pray as He leads you.

Occult / Witchcraft

It is important to take care of breaking off all witchcraft and renouncing any occult activity that you or anyone in your family line may have been involved in. The Following is a list of sins that the enemy could be using as an open door to attack you. You may choose to read through the list, and ask the Holy spirit to reveal to you which sins need to be dealt with, or just go through and renounce them all. Follow the leading of the Holy Spirit on this.

Prayer of Freedom

Heavenly Father, I confess, repent of, and renounce on behalf of myself, my ancestors, and my offspring, any involvement in:

__Animal / Human Sacrifice

__Astral Projection

__Alchemy

__Black or White Magic

__Blasphemy

__Spells or Hexes

__Chanting

__Channeling

__Conjuration

__Covens

__Drinking Blood or Urine

__Dispatching Demons

__Enchantments

__Evil Eye

__Fire Walking

__Grave Sucking

__Hallucinogenic Drugs

__Hexing and Vexing

__Trances (self or by others)

__Indian Occult Rituals

__Idolatry

__Incantations

__Levitation

__Meta Physics

__Magic Mantras

__Mind Control

__Non-Christian Exorcism

__Occult Control

__ Unholy Dedications

__Parapsychology

__ Telekinesis / Telepathy

__Psychometry (object reading)

__Pyramid Power

__Rebirthing

__Satanism

__Satanic Ritual Abuse

__Séances

__Sorcery

__Soul Travel

__Suicide

__Shape Shifting

__Table Tipping

__Transcendental Meditation

__Witchcraft

__Voodoo

Pause and repent of anything else the Holy Spirit reveals in this area. Then continue below.

Father, I confess on behalf of myself and my ancestors that we have sought knowledge outside of you. I understand that placing anything before you is idolatry and evil. I pray that you would help me to listen to your Holy Spirit directly and never turn to manmade objects, familiar spirits, or demonic rituals. On behalf of myself and my ancestors, I confess, repent of, and renounce the sins of:

__Astrology/ Zodiac

__Star Signs/Birth Signs

__Automatic Writing

__Clairvoyance

__Clairaudience

__Divination

__ESP Extra Sensory Perception

__Horoscopes

__Hand Reading

__False Tongues/False Gifts

__Fortune Telling

__Iridology

__I Ching (Yi Jing)

__Mediumship

__Mind Reading

__Omens

__Palm Reading

__Past Life Readings

__Pendulum Readings

__Psychic Healing / Prayers

__Psychic Readings

__Reading Tea Leaves

__Using Spirit Guides

__Necromancy (communicating with the dead)

__Non-Christian Dream Interpretation

__Seeking Witch Doctors

__Idolatry of Western Medicine (Pharmaekia)

Pause and repent of anything else the Holy Spirit reveals in this area. Then continue below.

I repent on behalf of myself and my ancestors for using any of the following objects or having them in our possession. Holy Spirit please show me anything that I might still have that I need to get rid of. I renounce all:

__Ankhs	__Hexagrams
__Chain Letters	__Magic Games
__Charms/Amulets	__Tarot Cards
__Talismans	__Ouija Boards
__Crystal Balls	__Pentagrams
__Crystals used for Power	__Rosaries
__Dream Catchers	__Eight Balls
__Divining Rods	__Pagan Objects
__Graven Images	__Occult Literature

Pause and repent of anything else the Holy Spirit reveals in this area. Then continue below.

Father, I realize that the enemy has crept into our culture and very demonic things have become popular and even labelled as harmless. I now understand that the following things are demonic and I want nothing to do with them. I repent on behalf of myself and my ancestors for any participation in the following:

__Anime	__Charlie Charlie

- __Bloody Mary ritual
- __Smudging (sage, incense, resins)
- __(the) Bell Witch
- __Dungeons & Dragons
- __Disney Witchcraft-Magic
- __Edgar Cayce
- __Imaginary Friends
- __Handwriting Analysis
- __Enneagram
- __Eastern Meditation
- __Greek Mythology
- __Halloween
- __Horror Movies
- __Hypnosis / Mesmerism
- __Karma
- __Light as a Feather Stiff as a Board
- __Martial Arts
- __Mardi Gras
- __Mermaids
- __Numerology
- __Poltergeists
- __Pokémon
- __Reiki
- __Red Door Yellow Door
- __Superstition
- __Trolls
- __Theosophy
- __Third Eye
- __Ungodly Tattoos
- __Ungodly Music
- __UFOs
- __Water Witching
- __Wizards
- __Yin Yang
- __Yoga
- __Zen

I ask you, Father, to break any rights, grounds, privileges or accesses that may have opened in my life as a result of this involvement. I ask you, Holy Spirit, to close and seal all doors that may have been opened to me and my offspring and to seal them with the blood of the Lord Jesus Christ. I choose to be obedient to your Word, Lord, and I place my confidence in you.

I ask your forgiveness on behalf of myself and my ancestors for seeking knowledge outside of you and for trying to control what only You should control.

I confess, repent of, and renounce all occult and ungodly supernatural involvement in my life and in the lives of my ancestors.

I break all oaths and covenants that have been made with the Kingdom of darkness knowingly or unknowingly by myself or my ancestors.

I bind and break every spell, every curse, every hex and every vex.

I declare the assignments, the curses and the powers flowing from those curses to be null and void.

I ask you Lord Jesus Christ to break all rights, grounds or privileges that these sins may have had in my life and in my offspring's lives. We will no longer live under their authority because we belong to Jesus Christ. I no longer want anything to do with these family sins. I ask you, Holy Spirit, to close and seal all doors that have been opened to me and my offspring. Seal them with the blood of the Lord Jesus Christ of Nazareth.

I bind every evil spirit associated with Witchcraft, False Religion, and the Occult and I cast it out now in the mighty name of Jesus. All evil leave me now. Leave my family now in Jesus' mighty name.

Pause and ask the Lord if there is anything else He would like you to pray or declare, and continue as the Holy Spirit leads you.

Now might be a good time to visit the "Examples of Spirits" section of this book. Ask the Holy Spirit to give you the gift of discernment of spirits and to reveal to you any that should be addressed directly by name and told to leave.

Involvement in Satanism

Prayer of Freedom

Lord, I ask you to forgive me and my ancestors for any involvement in Satanism. We choose to worship you and only you. I pray Lord that you would cleanse my bloodline of all satanic involvement. Purify us Lord, and deliver us from all evil associated with the worship of Satan. I confess repent of and renounce on behalf of myself and my ancestors ever knowingly or unknowingly:

- signing our name over to Satan or having had our name signed over to Satan

- any ceremony where we may have been wed to Satan

- any & all covenants that we made with Satan or that were made on our behalf

- all Satanic assignments for our lives, including duties, marriage, and children

- all spirit guides assigned to us.

- giving of our blood in the service of Satan

- eating of flesh or drinking of blood for Satanic worship.

- any and all guardians and Satanist parents that were assigned to us.

- any baptism in blood or urine whereby we are identified with Satan

- participating in any ceremony where we or others had sex with the Virgin Mary or with children

- making mockery of the Trinity by having reverse communion, reading the Scriptures in reverse, making a mockery of Holy Water, Holy Oil, or marking churches with Satanic Symbols

I break the power of all curses or vows that were made against us and any pronouncements or prayers that have been out of God's will for our lives.

I renounce all names and acts connected to Satanism referencing Satan or other spirits:

-The Goat	-Baal	-Arviat
-Morningstar	-Book	-Balak
-Satan	-Blood	-Daragon
-Prince of Darkness	-Urine	-Phoenix
	-Water	-Guardian
-Beelzebub	-Bread	
-Ark	-Motega	

I announce that:

- My name is now written in the Lamb's Book of Life (Revelation 3:5 / Revelation 21:27)

- I am the Bride of Christ (2 Corinthians 11:2 / Revelation 19:7)

- I am a partaker of the New Covenant with Christ with Jesus Christ and that I have been purchased and sealed through His shed Blood on the cross. (Revelation 5:9)

- God is my father and the Holy Spirit is my Guardian by which I am sealed.

- I have been baptized in Holy Spirit to Jesus Christ and that my identity is in Jesus alone. (Colossians 2:12)

- I have been ransomed by the Blood of the Lamb and that only Jesus Christ has authority over me, my family, my possessions, my job, my children and the generations. (Revelation 1:5-6)

- I commit myself to know and do only the will of God and accept only His guidance.

- I accept only the leading of the Holy Spirit and that God is my heavenly Father. (Galatians 4:6)

- I trust only in the shed blood of my Lord Jesus Christ.

- By faith I eat only the flesh and drink only the blood of Jesus in Holy Communion (1Corinthians 11:24-26)

- Christ has set me free from any and all condemnation and that I desire to follow His will for my life.

- I have been redeemed from all ancestral and other curses through the cross. It is no longer I who live but Christ Jesus who lives in me.

- I have been delivered from the kingdom of darkness to the kingdom of Light. I announce and release heavenly blessings into my life. (Galatians 3:13-14/2 Corinthians 5:17/ Colossians 1:13)

- I am totally free in Christ by the grace of my Heavenly Father through the working of the holy spirit by virtue of the shed Blood of Jesus', resurrection and His unceasing intercession. I share in the glory of our Lord Jesus. (John 14:23 / 2 Thessalonians 2:13-14/ Romans 8:34)

Pause and ask the Lord if there is anything else He would like you to pray or declare, and continue as the Holy Spirit leads you.

Secret Societies

Secret societies have been a way for the enemy to deceive people into making oaths and dedications to the Kingdom of Darkness without knowing the seriousness of what they are doing. If you or anyone in your family line has been involved in secret societies, you'll want to renounce them and be cleansed of any evil associated with them. Many fraternities and sororities even use ceremonies and rituals from other secret societies like Free Masonry.

Prayer of Freedom

Father in Heaven, I come to you seeking forgiveness and healing from all sins committed against you by myself or my ancestors. I honor my earthly father, mother, and ancestors. But, I completely turn away from and renounce all their sins, especially those that have exposed me [and my children] to any kind of harmful influence. I forgive all my ancestors for these sins and the effects that have come down to me. Lord, I ask you to cleanse me and my family of all iniquity and break every curse that has come down generationally because of it.

I renounce witchcraft, the spirit of the antichrist, and the curse of any demonic doctrine. I renounce idolatry, blasphemy, and all destructive forms of secrecy and deception.

I renounce the love of power, the love of money, and any fears that have held me in bondage.

Heavenly Father, I confess, renounce and reject on behalf of myself and my offspring, from now until Jesus returns, my involvement and the involvement of my ancestors in:

__Armstrong Radio Church

__Freemasonry

__Mormonism

__The Order of Amaranth

__Oddfellows

__Buffalos

__DeMolay Lodge

__Foresters

__Druids

__The Ku Klux Klan,

__Daughters of Eastern Star

__Daughters of the Nile

__The Grange

__Jehovah's Witnesses

__Jobs Daughter's Lodge

__The Woodmen of the World

__Riders of the Red Robe

- __The Mystic Order of the Veiled Prophets of the Enchanted Realm
- __The Way International
- __White Shrine
- __Rebekah's Lodge
- __Woodmen of the World
- __Masons
- __Moonies
- __Moose Lodge
- __Order of the White Shrine of Jerusalem
- __Eagles Lodge
- __The International Orders of Job's Daughters
- __The Rainbow Girls and the boys' Order of De Molay
- __Christian Education Society
- __Roman Catholicism
- __Knights of Columbus
- __Knights of Malta
- __Knights of Pythias
- __Knights Templar
- __Fraternities / Sororities
- __Religious Science
- __Christadelphians
- __Scientology
- __Christian Science
- __Odd Fellows Lodge
- __Orange Lodge
- __Order of the Arrow
- __Order of the Red Cross
- __Order of the Rainbow
- __Shriners

I renounce all spiritually binding oaths and rituals enacted in every level and degree of any of these organizations and any other secret society along with their destructive effects on me and my family.

I renounce the "Lewis Curse" against first-born sons and I break that curse and revoke its power in the name of the Lord Jesus Christ.

I renounce the blindfold and hoodwink and any effects they have had on my emotions and eyes, including all confusion and fears.

I renounce the noose around the neck, the fear of choking, and any spirit that causes difficulty in breathing.

I renounce the effects of all pagan objects and symbolism, aprons, books of rituals, rings and jewelry.

I renounce the entrapping of others and observing the helplessness of others during rituals.

I renounce the false communion, all mockery of the redemptive work of Jesus Christ on the cross, all unbelief, confusion and deception, and all worship of Lucifer as a god or bringer of enlightenment.

I humbly ask for your forgiveness, Lord Jesus, for myself and for my family line. Please purify our bodies, our spirits, our souls, our minds, our emotions, and our relationships.

In the name of Jesus Christ, I command all evil spirits that have attached themselves to me or to my family through secret societies to leave us and not return. The Lord rebuke you. Cleanse us, O Lord, with your blood and fill us with the transforming fire of your Holy Spirit.

Pause and ask the Lord if there is anything else He would like you to pray or declare, and continue as the Holy Spirit leads you.

Freemasons and their Descendants

Normally, I do not recommend very long prayers. I believe they are not typically necessary for deliverance, and it's too easy for people to start putting their faith in long prayers instead of the power of God.

However, with the issue of Freemasonry, I do believe it can be beneficial to go through and renounce all the oaths, covenants and dedications that you or your ancestors could have made knowingly or unknowingly over the years of involvement.

There is a Ministry called Jubilee Resources International that has a prayer that specifically renounces all the oaths and covenants and dedications made. You can find it at www.JubileeResources.org

I will warn that it is extensive and there is definitely some graphic language, because you'll be renouncing and breaking the power of things that are said in many of the rituals and ceremonies, but if you believe the Lord is leading you to pray further on this subject, I recommend you set some time aside to read through it and then pray through it preferably with your spouse and/or with another mature, Holy Spirit filled Christian present. Be led of the Lord in this.

Who should pray through this prayer?

The effects of this organization are in the majority of peoples bloodline in some form or another because it has been such a common deception worldwide for so long, and there are so many oaths, covenants, and dedications made at every level, right from the start. Freemasonry rituals have also branched out into so many other secret societies and organizations that may be seemingly innocent. Many people do not know what they are getting into at first, but they are deceived into making dedications to the kingdom of darkness through codes and fictitious names. Chances are, somewhere in your bloodline, evil has made its way in through Freemasonry. Dealing with this issue in the spiritual realm by the power of Jesus Christ and the revelation of the Holy Spirit, could be what brings breakthrough in so many areas that you've been needing it.

If the long prayer turns you off, then may I remind you of the prayer found in Nehemiah chapters 9-10 that the Israelites prayed confessing on behalf of themselves and their ancestors. It's a mouth full!

Again, the following website is where you will be able to find this prayer I am mentioning along with more information about Freemasonry and why you want to renounce it.

www.JubileeResources.org

Involvement in Religions

Have you or your ancestors been involved in any of the following religions that go against scripture? Check all that you know of or that the Holy Spirit reveals to you as being in your generational line.

__A S Spiritism
__Angel Worship
__Atheism
__Antisemitism
__Baha'i
__Black Muslim
__Buddhism
__Confucianism
__Demon Worship
__Druidry
__Eastern Mysticism
__Egyptian Paganism
__Eckankar
__Earth Worship
__Goddess worship
__Gaia Worship
__Greek and Roman Paganism
__Hari Krishna
__Humanism
__Hinduism
__Islam
__Inner Peace
__Indigo
__Jehovah's Witnesses

__Kabbalah
__Mormonism
__New Age
__Native American Religion/Spiritualism
__Norse Religons
__Paganism
__Pantheism
__Rastafarianism
__Reincarnation
__Roman Catholicism
__Rosicrucianism
__Spiritualism
__Satanic Worship
__Scientology
__Santeria
__Shamanism
__Shintoism
__Swedenborgianism
__Silva Mind Control
__Taoism
__Universalism
__Unitarianism
__Wicca

__Any other Religion that the Holy Spirit reveals to you

You can use the religions that you checked here to fill in the blank in the following prayer.

Prayer of Freedom

Heavenly Father, I repent on behalf of myself and my ancestors for participating in false religions and belief systems knowingly or unknowingly. I specifically confess, renounce and reject my participation and the participation of my ancestors in ___name of religion(s)__.

On behalf of myself, my ancestors, and my offspring, I renounce any prayers, ceremonies, traditions, baptisms, dedications, rituals, laying on of hands, blessings, food or drink, inhaling, prophetic words or beliefs of any religion or group where they stray from Your Word or the Truths of your Word. I ask you Jesus to come against any ungodly transfer of spirits in my life that may be connected to these false religious rituals and beliefs.

I ask you, Father, to break any rights, grounds, or accesses that may be in my life as a result of this involvement. I ask you, Holy Spirit, to close and seal all doors that were opened to me and my offspring and to seal them with the blood of the Lord Jesus Christ. I choose to be obedient to your Word and I place my confidence in You.

I ask your forgiveness on behalf of myself and my ancestors for seeking knowledge outside of you.

I confess, renounce and reject all occult and ungodly supernatural involvement in my life, the lives of my ancestors, and the lives of my offspring. I no longer want anything to do with these family sins.

I break all oaths and covenants that have been made by myself or my ancestors with the kingdom of darkness; knowingly or unknowingly.

I renounce and annul every covenant made with death by my ancestors or myself, including every agreement made with Sheol, and I renounce the all the lies and falsehoods which have been hidden behind.

I bind and break every spell, every curse, every hex and every vex. I declare the assignments, the curses and the powers flowing from those curses to be null and void. We will no longer live under their authority because we belong to Jesus Christ.

I bind every evil spirit associated with Witchcraft, False Religion, and the Occult and I cast it out now in the mighty name of Jesus. All evil leave me now. Leave my family now in the mighty name of Jesus.

Pause and ask the Lord if there is anything else He would like you to pray or declare, and continue as the Holy Spirit leads you.

Dedications

Participants that come from (or whose ancestors come from), Asia, Africa or Latin American those with American Indian ancestry, likely they or their ancestors have been dedicated to false gods and spirits that are really demons.

Those who have belonged to false religions such as Buddhism, Hinduism, Islam, Shintoism (Japan), or Shamanism (Korea), or to cults such as Freemasonry, Mormonism, Scientology, New Age, Christian Science etc. If their ancestors have belonged to such false religions, they should have the effects of dedications broken.

Prayer of Freedom

In the name of Jesus Christ my redeemer, I cancel any enemy rights and to break all power gained through dedications to false gods including _____. I cover all the rituals used in these dedications with the blood of Jesus Christ. Thank you, Lord, that I am redeemed by the blood of the Lamb, Jesus Christ, my Savior.

Dealing with the Spirit of Religion

It's possible that maybe you or your ancestors haven't been involved with any false religions or cults, but maybe you've been a part of a certain denomination or believed lies that have affected your relationship with the Lord. This can open the door to a spirit of religion in your life. The following prayer might be something you want to pray.

Prayer of Freedom

Father God, I come to you in the name of Jesus Christ your Son, and I confess on behalf of myself and my ancestors that we have given place to the spirit of religion in our lives. Forgive us Lord for not fully receiving your love, compassion, mercy, grace and forgiveness.

Forgive us for placing religious rituals, services, sacrifices, programs, and ideals, before you. Forgive us for believing the lie that you are distant, cold, judgmental, unloving, and unforgiving. I choose to embrace all aspects of Your true character and to intimately know You.

I repent on behalf of myself and my ancestors for relying on our own intellect in worship, praise, prayer, reading scripture, and spiritual warfare. I repent of and renounce all legalism, traditions and religious formulas. Forgive us Lord for all of our participation in dead works, dullness to the things of God, and hardness of heart. Forgive us for being complacent with dry religion instead of embracing the fullness of the deep and intimate relationship that you desire to have with us. Forgive us for allowing ourselves to be led by any other spirit than Your Holy Spirit, Lord.

I repent of and renounce not taking sin seriously, and even justifying it in my mind. Forgive me and my ancestors for being hypocritical and deceptive.

I repent of and renounce my lack of transparency with you Lord and with my fellow brothers and sisters in Christ. Forgive me and my ancestors for all the ways we've allowed pride, arrogance, and self-righteousness to deceive us into concealing sin, not receiving correction, and being defensive when confronted or rebuked by You or others.

I confess, repent of, and come out of agreement with, all comparison, judgement, criticism, gossip, jealousy, covetousness, anger, rebellion, control, manipulation, intimidation, and all persecution and slander of those moving in the Holy Spirit.

In the name of Jesus, I repent of and renounce every sin, known or unknown, that has given place to every spirit of religion in my bloodline. I ask you Father to break the curse of religion in my family line, and free us from all the confusion, sickness, and other bondage that it has caused. I declare that every right that religious spirits have had in my life are cancelled now by the power of Jesus' Christ and my personal relationship with Him. I renounce every spirit of religion and every work of darkness connected with it. I command every religious spirit, to leave me and my family now in the mighty name of Jesus.

Holy Spirit, fill me from the top of my head to the soles of my feet. Give me the ability to fully surrender to every plan that you have for my life. Help me to humbly obey and honor you and any Godly authority whom you have placed in my life. Help me to honor other leaders that I co-labor with and serve, without making them an idol in my life. Teach me how to be in healthy relationship with you and with others. In Jesus' name I pray.

Pause and ask the Lord if there is anything else He would like you to pray or declare, and continue as the Holy Spirit leads you.

Deeper Prayer About Specific Religions

If any of these religions have had a place in your life or in your family line. It might be a good idea to pray a little deeper about that specific religion. For instance, if you have a Roman Catholic background, the Lord may lead you to repent of and renounce things that go against scripture, like praying to dead saints, idolizing Mary, believing things that the Catholic church added to scripture, graven images, specific rituals, etc. If you are interested in some really great prayer guidelines for renouncing these practices you can find them at www.JubileeResources.org

They have helpful informational booklets and prayer guidelines for renouncing the practices in many religions such as: Roman Catholicism, Islam, Jehovah's Witnesses, Hinduism, Shintoism, New Age, Mormonism / Latter Day Saints, etc.

Native American Spiritualism

Father God,
I come to You on behalf of myself and all those in my ancestral line. I ask for Your forgiveness for our sins and rebellion against you. Forgive us for the worship of idols, people, animals, and other things in nature, when that worship should only be to you. I repent of and renounce on behalf of myself and my ancestors the sins of:

- using sage, tobacco, alcohol, and hallucinations for ceremonial or ungodly religious purposes
- ceremonial singing, chanting, and dances that involve the use of conjuring or connecting to ancestral spirits/demons

- using demonic power, psychic energy, ancient witchcraft practices, sorcery, charms, dream catchers, spells, incantations and magic.
- all customs of speaking word curses on our enemies through traditional songs
- ritually gambling and enticing others into a lifestyle of gambling
- soothsaying and shamanism

I renounce every familiar spirit guide and any and all other false gods and deities of various religions.

I renounce the demonic spirits of Native American Spiritualism, substance abuse, greed, gambling, addiction, idolatry, animal worship, and shamanism. I bind them all in Jesus' name and command them to leave me now. I renounce every spirit animal including the Black Bear, Wolf, Eagle, and any other animal that was worshipped by my ancestors. I command every demonic spirit associated with these animals and the worship of them to leave me and my family now and never return.

I renounce all practices of ritual and black magic, the Cherokee, Chickasaw, the Creek, Seminole, Choctaw, the Blackfoot, Cree, Crow, Pauite, Shoebone, Ojibwe, Cheyenne, Sioux, the Ute, Pawnee, the Navajo, Shawnee and Apache customs and traditions. I bind every demonic sprit associated with them and I command it to go in Jesus' name.

I ask you Father God to break every curse that these sins have brought upon my family. Have mercy on us and break every chain. Deliver us from all evil, I pray. I declare that the power of Jesus' has broken every chain. All nightmares must cease, all sickness must leave, in the mighty name of Jesus' Christ my king.

Pause and ask the Lord if there is anything else He would like you to pray or declare, and continue as the Holy Spirit leads you.

Reiki & Other Questionable Practices

The Lord has healed me and many others both supernaturally and by using natural means. There is nothing wrong with using the things that the Lord has given us in nature to heal. Many natural health and healing modalities are scientifically legitimate and beneficial.

The problem is when practitioners cross the line and start moving in the supernatural apart from Jesus Christ. This includes practices like Reiki, Therapeutic touch, hypnosis, mind control,

Chakra balancing, etc. This area can be tricky to navigate. You can go to a chiropractor who helps adjust and fix the subluxation in your spine, and then you can come across one who offers to "adjust your shadow." I once saw a practitioner who used a very scientific process to desensitize allergies. Then when we moved across the country, I tried to find someone else who did the same thing, and this practitioner started swinging a pendulum and telling she could send me healing from a distance. We could not get out of there fast enough!

I am all about alternatives to the conventional medical field, the Lord has used herbs, light, magnets, electrical stimulation and more to heal me from traumatic brain injury, but we have to be so careful to make sure we are led by the Holy Spirit and listen to the discernment that comes from Him. I've seen firsthand that things can get very weird, very quickly.

Ask the Lord if there have been any things that you have turned to for healing that were spiritually dangerous, and have opened the door to the enemy in your life. It is also important to note that even something good like vitamins and supplements can be a stumbling block if we look to it like an idol rather than use it only as guided by the Lord.

There may even be a practice that the Lord brings to your mind that might be good for someone else, but not for you. For instance, the Lord might use massage therapy to help one person, but to another it might be too much of a sexual temptation, or become an idol. Not to mention, the person who is giving the massage could also be a reiki practitioner carrying evil spirits, and now you have submitted to them to lay hands on you on their table. They could be calling upon spirit guides to help them massage you without your knowledge. I like to make sure that anyone I see for a massage is a strong Christian that I know well, and definitely doesn't practice any things like Reiki or Therapeutic Touch.

When it comes to the practical application of your health and well-being, only the Lord knows exactly what you should do or not, and that is why we need to continually seek Him. Doing this can also save you a lot of time and money, because He will guide you to the right treatments and therapies that will actually work for you. This is much better than just trying to figure it out on your own, wasting time and money on something that wasn't even what you needed, and could potentially open up the door to the enemy in your life.

Prayer of Freedom

Heavenly Father, I confess on behalf of myself and my ancestors that I have participated in ungodly healing practices including:

__Reiki

__Therapeutic Touch

__Chakra or Energy alignment

__Hypnosis

__The Higher Mind

__Higher Self

__Oneness

__Higher Consciousness

__Martial arts

__Yoga

__Transcendental Meditation

__Crystal Power

__Spirit guides

__Healing Angels

__Pendulum Swinging

__Universe Power

__Geometry healing

__Distance Healing

__Animist, Hindu, Confucian, Buddhist, Taoist or Ancient Knowledge/ Ancient Wisdom and Ancient Way philosophy and religion

__Allowing occult symbols to be traced on my body and over my spirit, emotions and mind

__All forms of Etheric and psychic surgery and manipulation, directly or indirectly applied through physical contact, meditation, projection or prayer.

__The opening of the Third Eye

__Seeking healing from practitioners of witchcraft who knowingly or unknowingly serve spirits of divination for knowledge.

__Recitation of all Mantra's, Taoist, Hindu and Buddhist meditations, prayers or philosophy, and the __Study of meridians and other energy lines or aura's

__Use of Sacred Words 'Om' and 'Sri', of emptying my mind and of any meditation practice where I have repeated any word or phrase in the process of seeking spiritual experiences.

__All symbols also placed by tattoo or body paint

__Allowing practitioners of witchcraft and unclean spirits to lay hands on me with my consent.

__Images and meditations of Ouroboros, Kundalini, Lotus position and Lotus flower, Diamonds and Prisms, crystals, walking of labyrinths and the Tree of Life for the use of centering or focus of my mind and spirit

__Acceptance of the 'O' and 'K' symbols traced for healing of spiritual wounds

__Anything else the Holy Spirit reveals to you

Father, please forgive me for entering the realm of evil, for welcoming and opening myself up knowingly or unknowingly to the devil's influences. I acknowledge that as a Christian, I should be led by the Holy Spirit and receive only His counsel of Truth. I now agree that through His power and guidance, I can be healed.

I repent of and renounce all agreements, vows, bonds and oaths made to all evil through these practices, whether these agreements have been verbal or implied by my active or passive tolerance and cooperation.

I take the sword of the Holy Spirit and cut the soul and spirit ties to all practitioners of these disciplines and refuse them all rights to continue to heal, align or influence my body, emotions or spirit. I ask you Lord that any healing symbols drawn on me would be removed.

In the name of Jesus, I repent and renounce all acceptance of the doctrines of demons and nephilim, of new gospels and new sources of wisdom and healing. I renounce all agreements with Chiron and Chironic Healing, and all agreements with Apollo, the Satanic false god of light.

I renounce the spirit of Kundalini, and the spirit of the Anti-Christ. I renounce all Greek and Hindu Gods and Goddesses and the demonic spirits associated with them.

I ask you Father to break every curse that may have come down the generations to me or the rest of my family. I command that the spiritual eye that marked my spirit and body during these therapies to now be closed.

I cancel and renounce every occult and magic symbol signed, written or otherwise designed over my body, skin and spirit by any Reiki master or practitioner. I ask You, Lord, to destroy these marks and cuts to the flesh, and I commit to not receiving any more.

I repent and renounce all marks and symbols placed on me (on my head, body or spirit) by any ungodly authority, priest or occultist and I specifically repent of and renounce receiving all false blessings and honoring by false prophets, teachers, faith healers, sages, gurus, shamans, martial arts masters, yoga instructors, witches, druids, and mystics. I now renounce and reject these in the name Jesus.

I now command every evil spirit associated with any healing practices that me or my ancestors have partaken in to leave me and my family now in the mighty name if Jesus.

Thank you, Lord, for showing me where I have gone astray. Holy Spirit, fill me and give the gift of discernment of spirits to help me recognize what is not of You. Help me to navigate correctly in this area of using what you have given us in nature for our bodies to heal, without opening the door to the enemy. In Jesus' name I pray. Amen.

Pause and ask the Lord if there is anything else He would like you to pray or declare, and continue as the Holy Spirit leads you.

If you were heavily involved in practicing or instructing some of the practices mentioned above, you may want to renounce the specific things that you did ceremonially that the Holy Spirit brings to your mind. Simply confess and renounce them out loud, in Jesus' name and tell every spirit associated with it to go.

Modern / Western Medicine

It's amazing how many people will be skeptical of any sort of natural health and healing modality, but yet they fail to see the evil in today's modern western medicine. The symbols for western medicine are the staff of Asclepius and the caduceus, or staff of Hermes, both of which are demonic.

Scripture says, multiple times, when the pagans sacrifice to their god's, they are not sacrificing to real gods, but to demons. Aslepius and Hermes are demon gods. The origins of western medicine come from pagan Greek culture. Aslepius was the Greek demon god of healing and medicine. There were healing temples set up in ancient Greece that were dedicated to this god and snakes were often used in the healing rituals. The caduceus which also has been adopted, as a symbol of western medicine is, oddly enough, strongly associated with trade, liars, thieves, eloquence, negotiation, alchemy, and wisdom.

In revelation we see this passage about the end times:

Revelation 28:23-24
"...and the light of a lamp will not shine in you any longer; and the voice of the bridegroom and bride will not be heard in you any longer; for your merchants were the great men of the earth, because all the nations

were deceived by your **sorcery.** And in her was found the blood of prophets and of saints and of all who have been slain on the earth."

I find it interesting that the Greek word translated to sorcery here is the word "pharmakeia" which means to minister drugs.

Just like with natural medicine, I believe there are still ways that God can use it to help us with our health and healing. However, I think more and more people are realizing that Western Medicine has brought more destruction on the health of our society than good. Science is reflecting that the average lifespan in America is decreasing not increasing, and one of the leading causes of death in America today is medical error.

As far as deliverance goes, I have seen just as many people need deliverance from practices associated with western medicine as I have seen needing deliverance from questionable alternative medicine. The deceptive ties go even deeper and are dangerously hidden. For generations, people have been raised to hold doctors in such high regard (which is the definition of worship) and do everything they say. Many Christians will do anything their doctor tells them to do, even to the point of taking multiple drugs and injecting all sorts of questionable substances into their bodies. Most do this without even first consulting the Lord! That is a very dangerous form of idolatry.

We have Christians in the church who are judging others for turning to alcohol or marijuana for relief when they themselves are depending on 5 different pharmaceutical drugs just to make it through the day. An addiction to drugs is still an addiction to drugs, even when it is paid for by insurance companies. When you step outside of the cultural conditioning that we have been being programmed with in this country, you start to see how messed up this mindset really is, and how much of a snare it can bring spiritually.

I recommend that you pause and ask the Lord if there are ways that you have idolized modern medicine and been trapped spiritually by it.

Prayer of Freedom

Heavenly Father, I confess the sin of my ancestors, and my own sin of idolizing western medicine, it's practices and practitioners. We have allowed people to make decisions for us about what we put into our bodies when our bodies are your temple and you should be the one to tell us what is appropriate to put in it. I repent of and renounce the use of pharmaceuticals to try to put a band aid on something that you want to completely heal. I repent of and renounce the use of drugs to numb pain either physically or emotionally, rather than seeking you for the root cause of the problem. I repent of and renounce the act of ingesting and injecting toxins including aborted fetal tissue into our bodies and those of our children. I ask you to heal me (and my children) and restore our bodies as if we had never partaken in theses harmful things.

I ask your forgiveness, Lord, on behalf of myself and my ancestors for not acknowledging you in all our ways, but looking to a person or organization for all of our answers, especially when that organization makes money off of me and my family being sick and uses the tissue of aborted babies for products.

I forgive my ancestors for these sins and for the consequences of them that have come down to my family and me I forgive my parents for any way that they have allowed things to happen to my body at the hands of medical practitioners that was not your will for me.

I forgive myself for any way that I have done the same to myself or my children. Lord, I ask you to forgive my ancestors and me for this idolatry and tolerance of evil. I ask Lord that you would break any curse this may have brought down to me and my family. In the name of the Lord Jesus Christ, and by His blood, I renounce all evil associated with the idolatry of Western Medicine. I renounce every Greek God associated with modern medicine and the demonic spirits behind them. I renounce and bind the spirit of Pharmakeia from having any power over me any longer. I break the power of every word curse that any practitioner has ever spoken over me. I renounce and rebuke every medical diagnosis that has allowed the enemy to have a place in my life or body. I do not receive these labels anymore, I do not let them define me. I command every evil spirit associated with these word curses to leave me now in Jesus' name.

Every Spirit of idolatry, every spirit of sickness and infirmity, and every spirit of Pharmakeia leave me and my family now and never return. I ask you, Holy Spirit, to close all doors that may have been opened to me and my offspring and seal them with the blood of Jesus. I break all evil generational ties from the beginning of time to the current generation, all evil spirits leave now and go to the abyss in Jesus' name.

Lord, I pray that you would touch my body right now with Your healing and cleansing power. Restore my health and make me whole.

Body, I command you to line up with the will of God and His perfect design for my health. Every abnormal cell be destroyed, and leave my body now. I declare that every cell in my body properly works according to its function given by my Creator. I command every hormone, every nutrient, every connection, and every chemical in my body to line up with the Word and the will of my Father in Heaven. God I thank you, that by the stripes of Jesus and the power of His death and resurrection, I am healed, I am whole, and I am restored completely, in Jesus' name. Amen!

Rejection

This is one of the most important sections of this book. I have yet to see someone who hasn't been touched by the power of God praying in this section. We've all faced rejection at one time or another, and so many other issues in life such as control, manipulation, fear, addictions, etc, can be rooted in rejection.

In this life, you will be rejected, but you do not have to carry a spirit of rejection. Take authority and tell that spirit to go today, and to take all of its problems with it.

I recommend that you really take the time to seek the Lord in this area. Are there ways that you have opened the door to the spirit of rejection by rejecting God or others? Has the spirit of rejection been tormenting you all of your life because of something that happened even while you were still in the womb? Ask the Lord to reveal every way that this ugly spirit has crept into your life and allow Him to deal with it for you today. Ask God to heal every wound. Let Him help you forgive everyone who has hurt you in this way. Allow the Lord to show you any way that you feel like He has rejected you and restore you from every lie that has had a stronghold on you.

Prayers of Freedom

Rejection of God

Father God, I come to you on behalf of myself and my ancestors, and I ask you to forgive us for all the times and all the ways that we have rejected You. I repent for not believing You, for not listening to You, and for refusing Your love. I confess that, at times, I have not trusted You and have doubted Your love for me. I confess that my ancestors and I have walked in stubbornness, pride, self-will, and rebellion. In the name of Jesus, I repent of, and renounce all rejection of My Heavenly Father, Jesus, and The Holy Spirit.

Please forgive me Lord, for all the ways I have quenched the power of the Holy Spirit in my life, by rejecting or refusing to use the gifts You have given me. Forgive me and my ancestors for not obeying the words you've spoken to us both written and spoken. I repent of, and renounce, trying to achieve righteousness or salvation by our own works of the flesh, thereby rejecting the gift of Salvation that Jesus paid for us.

I ask you Lord to forgive me and my ancestors for any way that we have been ashamed of our faith in you, and for anytime that we have denied you, or refused to stand for You in the face of persecution. I renounce and break all vows and covenants, soul ties, generational ties, and strongholds that would lead me to the rejection of

God. I choose to love the Lord my God with all my heart, with all my soul, with all my mind, and with all my strength. I renounce every spirit and break down every stronghold that has to do with the rejection of God. All evil associated with the rejection of God, leave me now in Jesus' name.

Pause and ask the Lord if there is anything else He would like you to pray or declare in this area then continue below.

Self-Rejection

Heavenly Father, I repent of and renounce on behalf of myself and my ancestors, all rejection of ourselves and refusing to accept who you made us to be. I repent for not believing that I have worth and value just as I am. I choose to accept myself, because you have wonderfully made me. I renounce all the negative things I have thought or said about myself and all the lies that I have believed about who I am or who I'm not. I break the power of all those curses and lies spoken or unspoken now, in Jesus' name. I break all ties with self-rejection, and every spirit or stronghold that would lead me to reject myself. Thank you for your forgiveness, Father and for showing me who I am in Christ.

Pause and ask the Lord if there is anything else He would like you to pray or declare in this area then continue below.

Fear of Rejection

Heavenly Father, I confess that my ancestors and I have given place to the fear of rejection in our lives. I repent of and renounce all lying, deception, suspicion, mistrust, control and manipulation, self-pity, and self-protective behavior that either I, or my ancestors have taken part in. I confess that I have tried to please people instead of You, Lord. I have based my decisions on the fear of man and fear of rejection instead of your love and commandments.

I choose to forgive _____ for rejecting me and all that pain that it caused. I pray, Lord, that you would help me trust You, and trust others again. Help me guard my heart, and keep it soft. I renounce the fear of rejection and all the destructive behavior it has led me into. I renounce and break all soul ties and generational ties to the fear of rejection, and break its hold in my life.

Father, I pray that you would rewire my brain for love; Your perfect love that casts out all fear. I ask you to cover me with the shalom peace that only comes from you.

Pause and ask the Lord if there is anything else He would like you to pray or declare in this area then continue below.

Rejection of Others

Heavenly Father, I confess on behalf of myself and my family line, the sin of rejecting others. I ask You to forgive us for all the hurt and pain that we have caused them. I repent of and renounce all unforgiveness, bitterness, anger, and resentment toward those who have hurt me or anyone I love. I ask you Lord to heal my soul of every wound. Help me truly forgive everyone who has rejected me in any way.

I repent of and renounce judging, blaming, and criticizing others and every thought or action of wanting to hurt them or tear them down. I repent of and renounce, all gossip and slander and all the ways I have allowed any spirit of rejecting others to influence me and my relationships. I renounce all soul ties, generational ties and every stronghold that has tied me to the rejection of others. I choose to walk in forgiveness toward everyone who has hurt me, and I ask you Lord to show me where I might need to ask for that same forgiveness from others whom I have hurt intentionally or unintentionally.

Pause and ask the Lord if there is anything else He would like you to pray or declare in this area, then continue below.

Dealing with the Spirit of Rejection

Father, I ask you to break every curse of rejection that has affected my family line, and deliver us of all evil associated with it. Every spirit of rejection, you are exposed and I renounce you. You have no right or authority to stay with me. I break all agreements with you. I renounce your lies and the fear and pain they've caused in my life. I sever all ties with you and I cast you out of my life. Every evil spirit of rejection, I command you to leave me now in the name of Jesus!

The ground the enemy has taken, I now take back, by the blood of Jesus. I am known, I am wanted, I am accepted, and I am loved by my perfect Father in Heaven. I am His child and He is my Abba (Daddy).

Pause and ask the Lord if there is anything else He would like you to pray or declare, and continue as the Holy Spirit leads you.

Guilt and Shame

Is the voice of condemnation and accusation strong in your mind? Are you constantly being reminded of your past and how it supposedly disqualifies you from living your purpose for God? You may need deliverance from guilt or shame. Guilt reminds you of your mistakes, shame makes you feel like you are the product of your mistakes, and even the mistakes of those who have hurt you.

Prayer of Freedom

Father God, I repent of doubting You and Your love for me. I also repent of not believing that You have really forgiven me. I declare that the blood of Jesus has cleansed me from all of the sin, all of the guilt, and all of the shame of my past. I repent of and renounce on behalf of myself and my ancestors, listening and agreeing with the voice of the "accuser" telling me that I am an evil person, that I am dirty, and that I am unworthy to come and receive Your love. It is not by my own works or righteousness, but the righteousness of Jesus that I am cleansed, healed and made whole. I love Him because He first loved me.

Lord, I ask you to forgive me and my ancestors for every way that we have shamed ourselves or others. Forgive us for every idle word spoken. I choose to forgive everyone who has shamed me, I now know that they were speaking out of their own brokenness, and the enemy was just using their pain to hurt me. I also choose to forgive myself for every failure, every sin, and all the destruction that has come from my sinful actions in the past. I declare that I am a new creation in Jesus Christ. The old is gone and the new has come. The Lord's mercies are new every morning and great is His faithfulness!

I renounce guilt, false guilt, shame, condemnation, self-condemnation, and all sense of unworthiness. I bind and renounce every evil spirit associated with them. I break all agreements I have made with the lying voices of these spirits. I renounce every negative statement that I have made about myself or others. I break the power of every curse spoken or unspoken that has come against me by way of others, or myself. I break all soul ties and all generational ties that would bind me in any way to past guilt, shame, or condemnation. I break every vow, covenant, or agreement that would give these spirits any power or influence in my life. I cast down every stronghold of the mind that has kept me in bondage. All spirits of guilt, shame, and condemnation, I break your power over me, in the mighty Name of Jesus. I command you to leave me and my family now and never return.

Father God, I choose to open my heart to receive Your unconditional love, Your grace, Your forgiveness, and a full release from all guilt, shame, and condemnation in my life. Help me to walk in victory, and understand that I am the righteousness of God in Christ Jesus!

Pause and ask the Lord if there is anything else He would like you to pray or declare, and continue as the Holy Spirit leads you.

Anger

The feeling or even emotion of anger in itself is not sinful or destructive. It is when we sin in our anger, and when a pattern of anger controls us that is the issue. Curses of anger and sprits of rage can be passed down the family line. I know this, because I have been delivered of a curse of anger that was passed down generationally. Wow, what a difference it has made to be walking in freedom from that for the past 14 years.

Prayer of Freedom

Father, I come to You right now, in the name of Jesus, and I repent on behalf of myself and my ancestors for any way that we have sinned in our anger or allowed anger to control our behavior. I break this family curse of anger, and I claim that it is not only broken, but also reversed in Jesus' name. I renounce every spirit of anger and rage, and I command them to leave me and my family now and never return. Thank you, Lord, for cleansing us of all unrighteousness. I release a blessing of joy and peace over my family. Holy Spirit fill us with your power, love and a sound mind. In Jesus' mighty name, Amen!

Pause and ask the Lord if there is anything else He would like you to pray or declare, and continue as the Holy Spirit leads you.

Abuse

This prayer will most likely have to be customized to fit your situation. You may have been abused, you may have been the abuser, or you may fit into both categories. Many times, people who abuse others, do so because they were abused and that opened the door for a pattern of abuse to ensue in their lives and in their family line. No matter how you have been connected or entrapped in patterns of abuse. You can break the power of that right now by forgiveness, taking authority in Jesus' name, and letting the Lord heal you.

Prayer of Freedom

Father in Heaven, I confess on behalf of myself and my ancestors for giving place to the spirit of abuse. I repent of and renounce all involvement with abuse or the spirit of abuse in my own life. I ask you Lord to forgive me and my ancestors for __Name any known specific things___. I choose to forgive _____ for abusing me and all the pain it has caused. I forgive myself for _____.

Lord, I ask you to heal my soul of all the wounds that abuse and trauma has caused and to touch and heal everyone else who may have been involved. Help me to fully heal and walk in forgiveness. I ask that you would restore everything that needs to be restored and severe everything that needs to be severed according to Your will. Help me walk in forgiveness and have healthy boundaries.

In the name of Jesus, I renounce and break every agreement with every spirit of abuse and trauma and I command you to leave me and my family now. I break all curses, vows, covenants, agreements, and strongholds, that have given you power in my life or in my family. I ask you Holy Spirit to close and seal all doors that opened me up to evil through trauma and abuse. Seal them with the blood of Jesus.

Heavenly Father, I ask you to break all ungodly ties or agreements to anyone who has abused or hurt me, even those I may not be aware of. I renounce all access and rights to me and my offspring because of the sin of my abusers and in the name of Jesus Christ of Nazareth I repent of and renounce all unholy reactions to any traumas or abuse I have experienced. All that does not belong to me I send it back to its source in its entirety. All that rightfully belongs to me, I ask You, Father God, to cleanse and return to me in its entirety.

I bind every spirit from sexual, physical, emotional, and mental abuse, in Jesus' name. All evil spirits associated with abuse must leave now.

Tell every spirit that the Lord reveals to you to go in Jesus' name. Some possible examples are below:

- Physical Abuse
- Mental Abuse
- Emotional Abuse
- Child Abuse
- Domestic Abuse
- Narcissism
- Rape
- Molestation
- Incest
- Hurt
- PTSD
- Rejection
- Insecurity
- Mind Control

- Domination
- Religious Abuse
- Unforgiveness
- Bitterness
- Hatred
- Anger
- Rage
- Wrath
- Temper
- Vengeance
- Retaliation
- Resentment
- Hopelessness
- Wounded Spirit

Father God, I ask you to heal my soul of every deep wound caused by abuse. I command all trauma to leave every cell in my body, all tension be released. I command new neural pathways in my brain to form and neurons to be wired for love and not fear, forgiveness instead of bitterness, in Jesus' name, Amen

Depression

It's not a sin to feel depressed at times. In fact, you are in good company with all the Prophets throughout scripture. Sometimes life can deal you some hard blows. Depression can be a physical illness as well as a mental state. A depressed physical state can affect your mind and a depressed mental state can affect how your body functions. We are spirit, soul, and body and rarely does anything affect us in only one of those parts. Things like depression and anxiety must be dealt with in all three categories for total freedom and healing. Ask the Lord today for the root causes of this depressed state you have been in. Has hope deferred made your heart sick? Is this an imbalance in your hormones or a nutrition deficiency? Is there a spirit of heaviness that has attached to you whether generationally, or through you believing a lie that something is hopeless? The Holy Spirit can guide you into all truth in this area. Wait on Him, and pray according to His guidance.

Prayer of Freedom

Father God, I repent on behalf of myself and my ancestors for every believing lies of hopelessness. I repent for any way that we have not taken care of our bodies as your temple. I confess and repent of not renewing our minds like Your Word says to do.

Pause and ask the Holy spirit if there is anything else that could have been an open door to depression in your family line and confess it. Then continue below.

I now confess these sins to You and claim through the blood of the Lord Jesus Christ, my forgiveness and cleansing of all iniquity. I ask you, Holy Spirit, to close and seal all doors that were opened to me, and to cancel all ground that evil may have gained. I break the curse of depression that has been over my life and anyone in my family line. I ask you, Lord, to heal every wound in my soul that could be tempting me to feel hopeless or depressed. I renounce all spirits of heaviness, and I put on the garment of praise. Lord, You are my rock and my redeemer. I will trust in you and rely on Your joy to be my strength. I command my body to line up with the perfect will of the Father and His design for my being. I command every vitamin level, every hormone level, and every chemical to be in balance according to the Lord's will for this season in my life. I command new brain cells to be created at a supernatural rate and new neural pathways to form. Brain, be balanced in Jesus' name according to God's perfect design for you, Help me Lord, to practically apply, in faith, all of your instructions for me, and to do my part in this healing process. I ask you to change my vision and perception of my life and my current situation. Help me see the good you are working in all things. I ask this in the name of my Lord and Savior Jesus Christ. Amen

Pause and ask the Lord if there is anything else He would like you to pray or declare, and continue as the Holy Spirit leads you.

Examples of Heaviness Spirits

Ask the Lord if there are any spirits you need to directly address and cast out. They might not even be on this list.

- Orphan Spirit
- Abandonment
- Rejection
- Self-Rejection
- Grief
- Neglect
- Outcast
- Loneliness
- Isolation
- Depression
- Unworthiness
- Despair
- Oppression
- Ridicule
- Anxiety
- Panic Attacks
- Bitterness
- Hurt

- Sadness   • Wounded   • Broken Spirit
                 Spirit   • Unforgiveness

Anxiety

It doesn't matter who you are, anxiety will try to make its way into your life at times. When it does, we need to be ready to resist it and trust in the Lord. The Bible says not to fear 365 times.

Anxiety can be a physical illness as well as a mental state. An anxious physical state can affect your mind and an anxious mental state can affect how your body functions.

We are spirit, soul, and body and rarely does anything affect us in only one of those parts. Things like depression and anxiety must be dealt with in all three categories for total freedom and healing.

Ask the Lord today for the root causes of this anxious state that you have been in. Has past trauma made your heart and mind fear the worst-case scenario? Do you have a hard time trusting in the Lord? Is this an imbalance in your hormones, a brain injury, or a nutrition deficiency? Is there a spirit of fear that has attached to you whether generationally, through trauma, or through your partnership with a lie? The Holy Spirit can guide you into all truth in this area. Wait on Him and pray according to His word.

Prayer of Freedom

Father God, I repent on behalf of myself and my ancestors for believing lies of fear from the enemy. I repent for any way that we have not taken care of our bodies as your temple. I confess and repent of, not renewing our minds like Your Word says to do.

Pause and ask the Holy spirit if there is anything else that could have been an open door to depression in your family line and confess it. Then continue below.

I now confess these sins to You and claim through the blood of the Lord Jesus Christ my forgiveness and cleansing of all iniquity. I ask you, Holy Spirit, to close and seal all doors and to cancel all ground that evil may have gained. I break the curse of fear and anxiety that has been over my life and anyone in my family line.

I ask you Lord, to heal every wound in my soul that has tempted me to feel fearful and lack peace.

I pray that you would heal my body and my brain of anything that is causing these feelings of fear or a lack of peace. Rewire my brain for love. I command toxic neural pathways in my brain to be destroyed and new neural pathways of love to be created. I declare that the Lord's mercies are new every morning and every day I have new brain cells and new healthy connections. I renounce all trauma in my past. I give it to you, Lord. I give you all my brokenness and I trust that you will give me beauty for these ashes.

I renounce all spirits of fear and every lie of the enemy that would tempt me to not trust the Lord completely with my life and the lives of those I love. Lord you are my rock and my redeemer. You are my fortress and my shield. I repent on behalf of myself and my ancestors for bowing down to an idol of self-protection. There is no way that we can fully protect ourselves or those whom we love. You are the only one we can trust to do that. I repent for holding against You, any time where I felt like you weren't there protecting me. I confess that I only see things through my small earthly perspective and by your power and grace, I choose from now on to trust that you see the big picture and you work good in all things for those who love You and are called according to Your purpose. Help me to see the ways that You have protected me and preserved me and worked good in every situation. Forgive me and my ancestors for the times that we have walked outside Your will for us and not abided in You and then blamed You for not protecting us; when it was us who rejected Your protection by our rebellion.

I declare that I will abide in the shadow of the Almighty, and I will dwell in His Shelter from now on, I will trust in the Lord and in the Power of His might. Help me Lord to obey Your commandments and rely on Your joy to be my strength.

I command my body to line up with the perfect will of the Father and His design for my being. I command every vitamin level, every hormone level, and every chemical to be in balance according to the Lord's will for this season in my life. Body I command you to come out of this pattern of fight or flight mode and into a restful state of peace and mental awareness. Help me Lord, to practically apply, in faith, all of Your instructions for me, and to do my part in this healing process. I ask You to change my vision and perception of my life and my current situation. Help me see the good You are working in all things. Fill me with your Shalom peace. I ask this in the name of my Lord and Savior Jesus Christ. Amen

Pause and ask the Lord if there is anything else He would like you to pray or declare, and continue as the Holy Spirit leads you.

Examples of Spirits of Fear

Ask the Lord if there are any spirits you need to directly address and cast out. They might not even be on this list.

- Fear
- Anxiety
- Trauma
- PTSD
- Restlessness
- Insomnia
- Fear of Death
- Fear of Loneliness
- Fear of Failure
- Fear of Success
- Evil Foreboding

- Nervousness
- Isolation
- Phobias
- Panic Attacks
- Mania
- Paranoia
- Striving
- Tension
- Suspicion
- Distrust

Performance / Perfectionism

Are you tired of constantly striving and never feeling like it's enough? Are you trying to earn the Father's love and respect? Are you living off of the affirmations of other people? This is a great prayer to break that bondage off. It is especially impactful for those who have been known as over-achievers or perfectionists to come to the Father, and let Him deliver them of this toxic way of thinking and every spirit associated with it.

Prayer of Freedom

Heavenly Father, I repent on behalf of myself and my ancestors for not fully receiving Your love for me and trying to perform in order to receive Your love. I repent of trying to achieve righteousness apart from faith in You. I repent of and renounce any pressures I have put on others to perform in order to receive my love and acceptance, and every pressure that I have placed on myself to earn love and acceptance from You or others. Forgive me and my ancestors Lord for placing value on ourselves and others based on performance. Help us to love and respect people for who they are, not what they can do. Help me to love and respect myself for who I am as well.

In the name of Jesus, I renounce the spirit of performance and every spirit associated with it. I renounce the lie of "never enough." I break every vow, renounce every lie, and tear down every stronghold of perfection and performance. I repent of and renounce all control, manipulation and criticism of myself and others. I take authority over all fear, worry, anxiety, and self-condemnation, and I command you to leave me now in the name of Jesus. I take the sword of the spirit, and I sever any connection with you and break your hold on my life, in the name of Jesus Christ.

I no longer receive shame and condemnation for not measuring up. I renounce and reject the lie that my self-worth is dependent upon my ability to perform. I announce the truth that my identity and sense of worth is found in who I am as God's child. Help me to stop trying to *act* like a child of the King, and just *be* one. I declare that I am adopted by grace into the family of the Most High, God and I understand that my performance does not cause my Heavenly Father to love me any more or any less. His grace is sufficient for me and His power is made perfect in my weaknesses.

I am already approved and accepted in Christ because of His death and resurrection for me. I choose to believe the truth that I have been saved, not by deeds done in my own righteousness, but according to the righteousness of Jesus. I choose to believe that I am no longer under the curse of the law, because Christ became a curse for me. I receive the free gift of life in Christ and choose to abide in Him. I renounce and reject striving for perfection by living under the law. Holy Spirit, close and seal all doors that may have been opened to me and my offspring. By Your grace, Heavenly Father, I choose from this day forward to walk by faith according to what You have said is true by the power of Your Holy Spirit, In Jesus' name Amen.

Pause and ask the Lord if there is anything else He would like you to pray or declare, and continue as the Holy Spirit leads you.

Sexual Issues

We live in a culture permeated with sexual sin, where even churches, are now compromising on the issue, but the Bible is clear about sexual sin. Here are just some of the things mentioned in scripture about the subject:

1 Corinthians 6:18 ESV
Flee from sexual immorality. Every other sin
a person commits is outside the body, but the
sexually immoral person sins against his own
body.

Hebrews 13:4 ESV
Let marriage be held in honor among all, and
let the marriage bed be undefiled, for God
will judge the sexually immoral and
adulterous.

Matthew 5:27-28 ESV
"You have heard that it was said, 'You shall
not commit adultery.' But I say to you that
everyone who looks at a woman with lustful
intent has already committed adultery with
her in his heart.

Ephesians 5:5 ESV
For you may be sure of this, that everyone
who is sexually immoral or impure, or who is
covetous (that is, an idolater), has no
inheritance in the kingdom of Christ and
God.

1 Corinthians 6:9-10 ESV
Or do you not know that the unrighteous will
not inherit the kingdom of God? Do not be
deceived: neither the sexually immoral, nor

idolaters, nor adulterers, nor men who practice homosexuality, nor thieves, nor the greedy, nor drunkards, nor revilers, nor swindlers will inherit the kingdom of God.

Leviticus 20:13 ESV
If a man lies with a male as with a woman, both of them have committed an abomination; they shall surely be put to death; their blood is upon them.

Romans 1:26-27 ESV
For this reason, God gave them up to dishonorable passions. For their women exchanged natural relations for those that are contrary to nature; and the men likewise gave up natural relations with women and were consumed with passion for one another, men committing shameless acts with men and receiving in themselves the due penalty for their error.

Leviticus 18:23 ESV
And you shall not lie with any animal and so make yourself unclean with it, neither shall any woman give herself to an animal to lie with it: it is perversion.

If we have participated in any sexual activity that goes against the word of God and His perfect design for our bodies, we need to confess, repent of it, renounce it and cast out all evil that is associated with it. When it comes to sexual sin, every part of our being is involved. It not only requires spiritual deliverance, but many times healing in your soul, renewing of your mind, and crucifying the flesh, even beating it into submission as Paul says in 1 Corinthians 9:27.

Our bodies are a temple of the Most High God and the enemy has always taken great pleasure in desecrating the Lord's temples. He wants you to be defiled, and a very common way he does that is through sexual sin, because the ties to our senses are so strong, the deception is so sly, and the slope is so steep.

Sexual sin is one of the most commonly mentioned in scripture, because it is one of the hardest to resist. The Bible actually says when it comes to this temptation to not necessarily stand, but to just Flee!

> 1 Corinthians 6:18-20
> Flee sexual immorality. Every other sin that a person commits is outside the body, but the sexually immoral person sins against his own body. Or do you not know that your body is a temple of the Holy Spirit within you, whom

you have from God, and that you are not your own? For you have been bought for a price: therefore, glorify God in your body.

This may require strict physical and mental boundaries to be put in place in your life. You may need to remove devices for a time, train your eyes to bounce from evil, and diligently train your mind to cast down imaginations. However, just implementing these things does not bring total freedom. Many Christians have been led to believe that they just have to modify their behavior and fight constantly all of their life. They've been told that it will always be a struggle and they will think about it all the time and never be able to overcome it.

Too many times, believers, clean up their act and put all these boundaries in place, but if the spirit, or curse, or soul wound is still there, the enemy will just wait for an opportune time of weakness, and then the person falls into the same sin over and over again. If the only reason that you aren't looking at pornography is because you don't allow yourself to use a computer or a tv, then what is going to happen the first time you find yourself alone in a hotel room with access to whatever channel you want? To many people think they are free, when in reality the enemy is just waiting for the right moment to use the open door he has to carry out His plan of destruction. This is where you see marriages and entire ministries fall to pieces.

In Christ, there is a better plan. A plan of deliverance, where you can actually be free of the root cause of what is making it so hard for you to turn from sexual sin. The following prayers will lead you through breaking the legal agreements that you and your ancestors have had with spirits of sexual sin, but don't just stop there. Ask the Holy spirit to give you the gift of discernment of spirits and tell you which spirit(s) to address and cast out of your life once and for all.

Does this mean you will never be tempted again? Of course not, there will be a time where eventually your flesh will have to be disciplined again, or a spirit will come back to look for an open door back into your life, but this time it will not be in you and have such a profound influence on your life. It will be an outsider trying to gain access, so you can more easily recognize it for what it is, and resist it with power. This is so much better than uncontrollably falling into the same sin over and over again. If you've been trying to clean up you act and find yourself constantly struggling, you probably have spiritual company that you need to deal with head on.

As you pray for deliverance in this area. Ask the Lord for revelation about any ways that you are being deceived into sexual sin. For instance, I have seen several times where a person has repented of pornography, but they were not willing to give up secular music. Most secular music (yes. even oldies) is created and sung by people who have given their lives to Satan for fame, and much of this music is sexually impure.

Even if you are not paying attention to the words, it is programming your non-conscious mind. Even if a specific song does not appear to be about sex or drugs, there can be a certain spiritual power in a song based on who is singing it to you. Let me explain it this way. Has the Lord ever touched you through music? Have you ever recognized a special anointing on someone to minister through music and when they minister you feel the presence of the Lord so strongly. Well, Satan counterfeits and perverts whatever the Lord does. He actually has people who are anointed to minister evil through music. I say all that to say this, if you are trying to get rid of sexual sin, but then you are still allowing yourself to listen to secular music written and sung by the devil's disciples who live lives of total depravity, (especially when it comes to acts of sexual impurity), you are leaving the door wide open to the enemy. Some will say that this is a bit ridiculous and it's just music and doesn't have that kind of power over a Christian. Then I will respond with this question. "If it has no power over you, then why is it so hard for you to give it up?" Whatever we know is dishonoring to God but is too hard for us to give up for Him, automatically has power over us. Also, when we submit ourselves to someone and give them a place to speak into our lives, whether they are a doctor, a therapist, or someone, singing a song over us, we are submitting to them and giving them a certain level of power or influence in our life. Be very careful who you allow to influence you.

Ask the Lord if there is anything deceptive that you need to be willing to give up to be totally free. This may require giving up a subscription to a health magazine, or not watching sports on television. Let the Lord guide you in these boundaries.

Also, I hope that you will allow the Lord to reveal anything he wants to root out of you to help you be free. Maybe you are a single person struggling with fornication. You've tried so hard to control your flesh, but the Lord might reveal to you in prayer that you need to be delivered of a spirit of rejection from a past relationship, or you need to be healed from wounds of abuse. In that case, pause this section and go deal with that, and then come back. Let the Lord decide your route of deliverance. He will reveal what He wants you to deal with and when, so that He can heal and deliver you from the root cause of whatever has kept you in bondage.

The Lord may also require you to confess out loud to someone. Especially when it comes to a sexual sin that can be so easily hidden. Everyone wants to pick on and judge the person that gets caught in adultery, or is known to be living with their girlfriend or boyfriend, but what about the many people who are committing adultery by looking at pornography or fantasizing about someone every day in secret. Sometimes our sin exposes us, but sometimes we bear the responsibility of exposing our sin and renouncing the things hidden because of shame.

I promise, if the Lord tells you to do something, no matter how bad you think the consequences will be, you're always better off obeying Him. Better to live with some temporary earthly consequences than to be tormented by demons and thrown in hell forever.

List of Sexual sins / open doors

Below is a list of sexual sins. Take time to ask the Holy Spirit which things need to be renounced. You probably know what things you've done but you may not know what your ancestors or past sexual partners have been involved with that could have influenced you in some way.

With a section like this, many people will choose to just confess it all, considering that it is likely that someone in their family was probably involved with most everything on the list in one form or another. We never want to face the fact that someone we know and trust could be involved in such evil, but we see time and time again that sometimes it's the most prominent and respected leaders in society that we find out were involved repulsive sin for years. When they are caught, everyone is surprised, but what about the sin or so many others that still lurks in the shameful darkness and no one sees but the Lord.

Just like every other section of this book, please rely on the Holy Spirit for revelation and navigation. There will be a list of spirits in this prayer for reference. Ask the Lord which one(s) should be addressed and cast out. He may reveal one that isn't even on the list. Just tell it to go in Jesus' name.

Prayer of Freedom

Heavenly Father, I confess renounce and reject on behalf of myself and my ancestors the sins of:

__Adultery	__Masturbation
__Bestiality	__Molestation
__Bisexuality	__Pedophilia
__Cybersex	__Perversion
__Defilement	__Pornography
__Demonic Sex	__Premarital Sex
__Erotica	__Promiscuity
__Exposure	__Prostitution/Harlotry
__Fantasy	__Rape
__Lust	__Sadism
__Fornication	__Seduction/Alluring
__Frigidity	__Sexual Abuse
__Homosexuality	__Sodomy
__Illegitimacy	__Succubus
__Incest	__Uncleanness
__Incubus	__Voyeurism
__Lesbianism	__Human trafficking
__Masochism	

__Anything else Holy   Spirit reveals to you

I forgive my ancestors for these sins and for the consequences of the iniquity that have come down to my family and me. I forgive myself for any way that I have participated in these sins. Lord, I ask you to forgive my ancestors and me for these shameful acts. I no longer want anything to do with this sin, and I ask you to sever all ties that have bound me to it in any way.

In the name of Jesus, I renounce and reject all ungodly sexual sin in all its forms in my life, and I ask you, Holy Spirit, to close and seal all doors to my life, and my offspring, with the blood of the Lord Jesus Christ. Father, I ask you, with Jesus as my advocate, to break every generational curse associated with these sexual sins. I ask you to cleanse me of all iniquity and deliver me of all evil associated with it. I ask You to cleanse and bless my bloodline, Father, in Your goodness and mercy.

Deliver me of all shame, guilt and condemnation that the enemy has tried to put on me because of my past. I bind all evil spirits associated with these sexual sins and command them to leave me now, in the mighty name of Jesus.

Ask the Lord which one(s) you may need to tell to leave. Here are some examples:

- Incubus
- Succubus
- Pornography
- Masturbation
- Seducing Spirits
- Nakedness
- Fornication
- Adultery
- Divorce
- Illegitimacy
- Homosexuality
- Lesbianism
- Feminism
- Bisexuality
- Bestiality
- Whoredom
- Sadism
- Masochism
- Harlotry
- Prostitution
- Pedophilia
- Fantasy
- Transgenderism
- Gender Dysphoria
- Spirit Spouses (divorce them out loud)
- Fetishes
- Bondage
- Lewdness
- Oral Sex
- Perversity
- Filthy Imagination
- Foul
- Sensual
- Effeminate
- Flirtation
- Inordinate Affection
- Unnatural Affection
- Lasciviousness
- Promiscuity
- Sexually Transmitted Diseases
- Defilement

Lord, please restore a godly sexuality to me, and may I look to you to fulfill all my needs. Help me to guard my mind and my heart. Help me to crucify my flesh, and discipline my mind. I pray that you would fill me to overflowing with Your Holy Spirit and guide me in my daily choices; helping me to set boundaries and resist all temptation. In Jesus name, Amen

Pause and ask the Lord if there is anything else He would like you to pray or declare, and continue as the Holy Spirit leads you. This might be a good time to visit the "Examples of Spirits" section and also the "Soul Ties" section. Ask the Holy Spirit to reveal any other spirit that needs to be addressed and cast out.

Adultery/Fornication

Any sexual involvement outside of marriage is ungodly and opens the door to destruction. Take some time to ask the Lord what might need to specifically be renounced and broken or restored.

Prayer of Freedom

Heavenly Father, I, __your name__ acknowledge, confess and take full responsibility for sexually sinning when I participated in ungodly sexual involvement with ____partners names____.

I repent on behalf of myself and my ancestors for all ungodly sexual involvement with people we had no business being tied to, and I ask you to forgive me and my ancestors for sinning against you and against our own bodies. I forgive my ancestors for setting me up for this sin. I forgive myself for participating in this sin and I forgive the people who have also participated with me in this sin, enticed me or deceived me into sinning in this way. I receive your forgiveness, Lord.

In the name of Jesus, I renounce and reject all ungodly sexual sin in all its forms in my life, and I ask you, Holy Spirit, to close and seal all doors to my life, and my offspring, with the blood of the Lord Jesus Christ. Father, I ask You to break every generational curse associated with these sexual sins. I ask you to cleanse me of all iniquity and deliver me of all evil associated with it.

I break every soul tie and bonding of flesh that occurred because of this sin. I ask you Lord, to severe every ungodly connection that has crept into my life because of sexual sin. I ask you to break any bondage or foothold that evil may have obtained through this involvement. Please remove from me all that does not belong to me and send it back to its source. Please cleanse and return all that rightfully belongs to me, and restore to me what has been lost.

I ask you Lord, to cleanse my mind, body and soul. Please restore a godly sexuality to me. I now commit to being obedient to your holy ways. Help me to keep my body and mind holy. Purify me now Lord Jesus I pray.

Pause and ask the Lord if there is anything else He would like you to pray or declare, and continue as the Holy Spirit leads you.

Sexual Power and Deception

Sex is a powerful motivator and can too often be used as a means to manipulate others. If you have fallen into this trap, here is a place to repent.

Prayer of Freedom

Father in Heaven, I confess, renounce and reject on behalf of myself and my ancestors, all forms of sexual power and deception that we have used to gain influence, control and power over others, men or women. I ask your forgiveness for all the ways I have acted this out in my life. I no longer want anything to do with this unholy and demonic power. I command every spirit of sexual deception and power to leave me now in the mighty name of Jesus. Holy Spirit, I ask you to close and seal all doors that may have been opened to me and my offspring because of this sin. Cleanse my bloodline Father God, and break every curse associated with this witchcraft. Lord, I ask you to restore to me a holy and righteous sexuality. In Jesus' name I pray.

Pause and ask the Lord if there is anything else He would like you to pray or declare, and continue as the Holy Spirit leads you.

Molestation Rape Incest

If you need freedom from sexual abuse, and any ungodly reactions to trauma or abuse, continue below.

Prayer of Freedom

Heavenly Father, I ask you to break all ungodly ties or agreements to anyone who has abused or hurt me, even those I may not be aware of. I renounce and reject all access and rights to me and my offspring because of the sin of my abusers. In the name of Jesus, I renounce any ungodly reactions to any traumas I may have experienced - even those I may not be aware of.

I choose to forgive _____ for _____ and all the pain that it has caused me. I now understand that they were just broken people being used as pawns in the enemies plans to destroy me, but I have been redeemed by the blood of the Lamb. Holy spirit, give me the power to continue to walk in forgiveness. I pray that everyone who has abused me, would be saved, healed, delivered, and set free.

In the name of Jesus, I renounce and break every agreement with every spirit of rape, incest, molestation, abuse and trauma, and I command you to leave me and my family now. I break all curses, vows, covenants, agreements, and strongholds, that have given you power in my life or in my family.

Holy Spirit, I ask you to close and seal all doors that opened me up to evil through trauma and sexual abuse of every form. Seal them with the blood of Jesus.

Holy Spirit, I also ask you to remove from me all that does not belong to me, and send it back to its source. Please cleanse and return all that rightfully belongs to me and restore to me what has been lost. Continue to heal me and cleanse me, mind, body and spirit. I ask you to heal my soul of every deep wound caused by abuse. I command all trauma to leave every cell in my body, all tension be released. I command new neural pathways in my brain to form and neurons to be wired for love and not fear, in Jesus name, Amen

Pause and ask the Lord if there is anything else He would like you to pray or declare, and continue as the Holy Spirit leads you.

Homosexuality

This is a sensitive topic in today's culture. It seems the American church is somewhat polarized. In some churches the sin of homosexuality is allowed and even celebrated, in others, people who struggle with this sin are treated horribly as if it's a different category of sin than all others. If you have been struggling with homosexuality in your life, I would encourage you not to look to the opinions of other Christians for your example of how the Father feels towards you. Run straight to Him, and let Him, in His perfect love, mercy and compassion, heal you of every wound. He knows everything that you have been through. He sees the trauma and the pain. If you have suffered abuse, I encourage you to back up one prayer and start with that. First, let the Lord heal you, and then in His kindness, lead you to repentance and restoration of your sexuality.

Prayer of Freedom

Heavenly Father, I renounce the lie that You have created me or anyone else to be homosexual, and I affirm that You clearly forbid homosexual behavior. I accept myself as a child of God and declare that You created me and my sexuality in your perfect design. I confess on behalf of myself and my ancestors any involvement and any experimentation in homosexual practices or behaviors. I ask for your forgiveness, Lord. I also renounce any bondages or strongholds that have perverted my relationships with others.

I announce that I am free to relate to my same sex in the way that You intended. Lord, I ask you to break every curse and loose every chain associated with homosexuality in all its forms. Cleanse me, heal me and restore me spirit, soul, and body. I command my mind and my body to align with God's perfect design for sexuality. Every cell in my body must line up with the word of God and His perfect design for sex. Every hormone in my body, be balanced in Jesus' name.

Holy Spirit, I ask you to close and seal all doors and openings to my life and my offspring. Please restore a godly sexuality to me and help me to renew my mind with God's Word and God's Truth. In Jesus name, Amen.

Pause and ask the Lord if there is anything else He would like you to pray or declare, and continue as the Holy Spirit leads you.

Sexual Identity

This is a sensitive topic in today's culture. It seems the American church is somewhat polarized. In some churches gender confusion is tolerated and even celebrated, in others, people who struggle with it are treated horribly as if it's a different category of sin than all others. If you have been struggling with gender identity, I would encourage you not to look to the opinions of other Christians for your example of how the

Father feels towards you. Run straight to Him, and let Him, in His perfect love, mercy and compassion, heal you of every wound. He knows everything that you have been through. He sees the trauma and the pain. If you have suffered abuse, I encourage you to go a couple prayers back to the abuse section and start there. First, let the Lord heal you, and then in His kindness, lead you to repentance and restoration of your sexuality.

Prayer of Freedom

Heavenly Father, I confess, renounce and reject on behalf of myself and my ancestors all struggle with sexual identity and all the ways we have acted this out in our lives. I forgive myself for this sin against my body and I forgive any others who were involved in influencing this sin in my life. I ask for your forgiveness Lord. Help me to receive it and receive your true love for me. I pray that you would heal my physical body of anything that would be contributing to sexual identity issues and gender confusion. Heal and restore my DNA, my chromosomes, and every cell in my body. I command my hormones to line up with the will of God and His perfect design for me.

Father, I pray that you would break every stronghold of the mind and generational curse of confusion. Please deliver me of all evil that has been tormenting my mind. I command all evil spirits associated with my sexual identity and gender confusion to leave me now in the mighty name of Jesus.

Holy Spirit, please close and seal all doors to my life that the enemy was using to attack me and my mind. Jesus, I ask you to restore my true sexual identity to me. Continue to show me what this means in my life. I ask you to bless my gender and my sexuality, and I thank you for creating me in your image Lord. Help me to love who you created me to be. Help me to fully enjoy the gender that you have blessed me with. In Jesus name, Amen.

Pause and ask the Lord if there is anything else He would like you to pray or declare, and continue as the Holy Spirit leads you.

Divorce

If you have been through the pain of divorce, or if you notice a pattern of divorce in your family that the Lord is leading you to break, continue below.

Prayer of Freedom

Heavenly Father, I confess to you on behalf of myself and my ancestors any part that we have played in divorce.

Ask the Lord to show you specifics.

I choose to forgive my ancestors, myself, and our ex-spouses. Help me walk in this forgiveness, and I ask you Lord to forgive me (or my ancestors) for _____.

I renounce the lie that my identity is now in "being divorced." I declare that I am a child of God, and I reject the lie that says I am a 2nd class Christian because of my divorce. I reject the lie that says I am worthless, unlovable, or that my life is empty and meaningless, I am complete in Christ who loves me and accepts me.

I ask you Lord to continue to heal me and cleanse me spirit, soul, and body. I pray that I would be satisfied by your love and other godly relationships in my life. Help me to be okay with whatever your will is for my life and my relationships. I ask that you would sever every ungodly soul tie in my life that may be causing destruction. Return to me what is mine, and return to them all that is theirs. Make me whole, I pray.

I ask you Father, to cleanse my bloodline and break every curse of divorce. I ask that you would restore Godly relationships in my family.

In Jesus' name, I command every evil spirit associated with divorce to leave me and my family now. Thank you, Father, for healing my soul of every wound. Thank you for restoring trust in my life and help me to look to You to fulfill all of my emotional needs, because you are the only perfect One who can.

Pause and ask the Lord if there is anything else He would like you to pray or declare, and continue as the Holy Spirit leads you.

Miscarriages

Sometimes the enemy can gain unfair access to us during trauma, none of which is your fault. This is war and the enemy does not fight fair. Ask the Lord if there was any root cause of miscarriage that he wants to deliver you of or if the miscarriage somehow opened the door for the enemy to attack you further.

Prayer of Freedom

Heavenly Father, I confess and repent of, on behalf of myself and my ancestors all sin, idolatry, abuse, unforgiveness, freemasonry, abortion, jealousy, or anything else that could have caused an open door for the enemy to cause infertility or miscarriage in my life.

If the trauma of miscarriage has opened me up in any way to the kingdom of darkness, I ask you Holy Spirit, to close and seal all doors that may have been opened to me and my offspring.

I pray that you would cleanse me of all iniquity that has come down to me, and break every curse of infertility, miscarriage, and premature death. I command every evil spirit associated with any of these curses or incidents to leave me now in the mighty name of Jesus. Lord, heal my soul. Heal my body. Help me trust again. I command all fear of loss to leave me now in Jesus' name. Lord, help me be content in my family situation, and if it is Your will that I have another child, I pray that I would have a supernatural peace that only comes from you. I pray that I would enjoy my pregnancy without fear. Thank you, that I will be reunited

with my child(ren) one day in Heaven. In Jesus'
name, Amen.

*Pause and ask the Lord if there is anything else He would
like you to pray or declare, and continue as the Holy Spirit
leads you.*

Soul Ties

When we bond with someone in an intimate way,
a soul tie can be formed. This is in Gods design
and healthy. A husband and wife in a godly
marriage is a good soul tie, just like a healthy
mother and child relationship, and so on. When
we break free of sin, betrayal, trauma, abuse and
idolatry, we may need to break ungodly soul ties
that were formed. This includes, but is not limited
to, adultery and any sexual partners outside of
marriage. It could also be an ex-spouse, a former
best friend, someone or something that you
idolized, etc. Ask the Lord to reveal if there are
any soul ties in your life that need to be broken or
any bonding of the flesh that needs to be severed.

> 1 Samuel 18:1
> As soon as he had finished speaking to Saul,
> the soul of Jonathan was knit to the soul of

David, and Jonathan loved him as his own soul.

1 Corinthians 6:16 ESV
Or do you not know that he who is joined to a prostitute becomes one body with her? For, as it is written, "The two will become one flesh."

Prayer of Freedom

I, _____, renounce the soul tie I have with _____, and I ask you Jesus, to break any power that evil may have gained over me through this relationship. Father God, I ask you to break all ungodly soul ties and sever any bonds of flesh to these individuals. Jesus, remove all from me that belongs to them and cleanse and return all that rightfully belongs to me. Holy Spirit, I ask you to close and seal all doors to me and my offspring that may have been opened through this ungodly connection.

Father God, I repent of and renounce all immoral sexual activity in which I have participated. I renounce all idolatry and all toleration of evil, and I renounce all unclean spirits behind these acts.

Lord, I ask You to forgive me and cleanse me of all bondage in my life that happened because of these sins. I renounce every lie of the enemy telling me that I am dirty or that I am unacceptable because of my past sexual activities or abuse.

I also choose to bring all memories of past sexual involvement under the covering of the blood of Jesus. I repent on behalf of myself and my ancestors of making someone else's approval and acceptance of us more important than Yours. I repent of any way I have desired someone's love more than Yours. I repent of any way I have made any person or thing an idol in my life. I confess the sins of idolatry in my former generations, and I repent of all idolatry in my own life.

I renounce all unholy emotions, soul ties and ungodly bonding of the flesh. I renounce all the lies from the enemy that have made me look to others for my comfort, my sense of worth, or value. I renounce and separate myself from all idolatry in my family line. In Jesus' name, I take authority over all spirits of sexual sin and idolatry and I break their hold in my life. You will not keep me emotionally bound any longer. I command you to leave me now. I ask you Lord to heal my body and soul of all damage that these ties or bonds have caused. Father I ask you to pick up the shattered pieces of my soul purify them, and knit them back together. Make me whole, I pray. I give you all the glory for my healing.

Thank you, Lord Jesus, that You fully accept me and love me unconditionally. I choose to put You first in my life and at the center of everything I do and believe. I now present my body to You as a living sacrifice, and I ask that You fill me to overflowing with Your Holy Spirit.

Pause and ask the Lord if there is anything else He would like you to pray or declare, and continue as the Holy Spirit leads you.

Harming Self or Others

Matthew 22:37-39
And He said to him, "'You shall love the Lord your God with all your heart, and with all your soul, and with all your mind.' This is the great and foremost commandment. The second is like it, 'You shall love your neighbor as yourself.'

Addictions / Substance Abuse

Overcoming addiction is a multi-faceted battle. The spirit, soul, and body must all be addressed. Spiritual bondage must be broken, soul wounds must be healed, new neural pathways must be formed, new habits must be created, and many times even a new community of friends must be found.

There are no shortage of self-help programs and medical treatment centers, but they miss out on the very important spiritual factor. Many times, people will address the spiritual, but only try to cast out a spirit of addiction. They don't realize that addiction is often times rooted in other issues that result in an addiction to try to numb the pain. Let the Lord reveal every root cause and maybe even take you back to the table of contents to show you what else to pray through, before or after this prayer. What He says may surprise you. It could be that He wants to heal something you thought you were over, but it was never properly dealt with, etc.

Prayer of Freedom

Heavenly Father, I confess on behalf of myself and my ancestors for turning to substances to fill the void that only you can. I confess, repent of and renounce my struggle with __(name of addiction)__ in all its forms, and all the ways I have acted this out in my life. I ask you Jesus to forgive me for using _____ to meet my needs. Help me to receive your forgiveness. I renounce and reject any satanic connection or influence in my life through my misuse of chemicals or food. I ask you, Holy Spirit, to close and seal all doors to my life and my offspring that were opened to me by partnering with addiction, or that caused addiction to be a struggle in my life in the first place. I cast my anxiety onto Christ who loves me, and I commit myself to no longer yield to substance abuse but to the Holy Spirit.

Father, I ask you to heal me of the wounds in my soul that have tempted me to numb the pain of my past. I ask you as the just judge to cleanse my generational line of all iniquity and break every curse of addiction in my family. I command every evil spirit associated with addiction and substance abuse in all its forms to leave me now in the mighty name of Jesus and never return.

I ask You, Lord, to fill me with Your Holy Spirit form the top of my head to the soles of my feet.

Give me to power to resist temptation. I speak to my body in Jesus' name and I command it to be healed. Lord, restore my body and heal me as if I never put these substances in my body.

Pause and ask the Lord if there is anything else He would like you to pray or declare, and continue as the Holy Spirit leads you.

Shedding of innocent blood

Proverbs 6:16-19
There are six things which the Lord hates,
Yes, seven which are an abomination to Him:
17 Haughty eyes, a lying tongue, And hands that shed innocent blood,
18 A heart that devises wicked plans, Feet that run rapidly to evil,
19 A false witness who utters lies, And one who spreads strife among brothers.

Abortion

If you have been through the pain of abortion whether it was performed on you or you were a part of it being performed on another person, continue to pray below.

Prayer of Freedom

Heavenly Father, I, _____ acknowledge, confess and take full responsibility for having (an) abortion(s). (or for supporting _(woman's name)_, to have an abortion). I am sorry for taking the life of my unborn child(ren), and I ask you for your forgiveness. Help me to receive this forgiveness that only You can give. I recognize that you, Lord God, are the giver and the taker of life. I renounce this act of abortion on behalf of myself and my offspring. I ask you Lord to also forgive any of my ancestors who have shed innocent blood in any way. Please break any generational curse that this could have caused. I command every spirit associated with these sins of shedding innocent blood to leave me and my family now and never return. I ask you, Holy Spirit, to close and seal all doors to my life, and my offspring, seal them with the blood of Jesus. I ask you, Holy Spirit, to continue to bring healing to my soul and my body in this area. In Jesus' name I pray.

Pause and ask the Lord if there is anything else He would like you to pray or declare, and continue as the Holy Spirit leads you.

Murder / Assault

If you have been involved with murder or assault in any way, or you know this was somewhere in your family line, continue to pray below.

Prayer of Freedom

Heavenly Father, I confess on behalf of _myself/ancestors_ for the horrible acts of murder or assault. I forgive my ancestors for the sin and for the consequences of the sin that have come down to my family and me.

Self: I confess that I have _____. I ask you Lord in your mercy to forgive me for sinning against this person and against you.

Ancestors only: Although, I may not have personally taken part in these sins, I understand that there is a need to recognize the sins of those that came before me and I ask for the blood of Jesus to atone for these things so that my family bloodline can be cleansed.

Father, I ask you to break every curse of death and destruction that has come down to be because of these sins.

I forgive myself for any way that I have participated in this sin or in the sin of hatred toward others. Lord, I ask you to forgive my ancestors/me for the shedding of innocent blood and for all hatred we had had for others.

In the name of the Lord Jesus Christ, and by the power of His death and resurrection, I renounce all evil associated with murder or assault. I ask you, Holy Spirit, to close all doors that may have been opened to me and my offspring and seal them with the blood of Jesus. I break all evil generational ties from the beginning of time to the current generation, all evil spirits leave now and go to the abyss in Jesus' name. Amen!

Pause and ask the Lord if there is anything else He would like you to pray or declare, and continue as the Holy Spirit leads you.

Eating Disorders

If you have dealt with an eating disorder or exercise disorder at any point in your life or if they have run in your family line, continue praying below.

Prayer of Freedom

Heavenly Father, I confess on behalf of myself and my ancestors that we have misused and abused our bodies. I now understand that my body is a holy temple and to treat it as such. I renounce the lie that my value as a person is dependent upon my physical beauty, my weight, or size. I confess, repent of and renounce, vomiting, using laxatives, or starving myself as a means of cleansing myself of evil or altering my appearance.

I announce that only the blood of the Lord Jesus Christ cleanses me from sin. I accept the reality that there may be sin present in me due to the lies I have believed and the wrongful use of my body, but I renounce the lie that I am evil or that any part of my body is evil. I ask you Lord to cleanse me of all iniquity and break every curse that would lead me to harm my body; or that was caused by me choosing to harm my body. I command all evil associated with anorexia, bulimia, or any other eating or exercise disorder to leave me now in the mighty name of Jesus.

Father, I receive Your perfect love and acceptance of me. Help me to love myself as I am and receive everything you have designed and created me to be. Holy Spirit, I ask you to close and seal all doors that may have been opened to me and my offspring. Seal them with the blood of the Lord Jesus Christ. Amen.

Cutting / Other Self Harm

If you have dealt with cutting or other self-harm at any point in your life or if these things have run in your family line, continue praying below.

Prayer of Freedom

Heavenly Father, I confess on behalf of myself and my ancestors that we have misused and abused our bodies. I now understand that my body is a holy temple and to treat it as such. I confess, repent of, and renounce cutting myself, starving myself, hitting myself, or _any other self-harm_.

I pray Lord that you would deliver me of all evil and heal my soul of every wound that would tempt me to harm and abuse myself. I accept the reality that there may be sin present in me due to the lies I have believed and the wrongful use of my body, but I renounce the lie that I am evil or that any part of my body is evil. I confess, repent of and renounce all self-hatred, and self-rejection.

Lord. I receive Your love and acceptance of me. Help me to accept and love myself and my body as the holy temple that you have created it to be. I ask you Father God, to break every curse associated with self-hatred and self-harm. I command every evil spirit associated with these sins to leave me now and never return. Holy Spirit, I ask you to close and seal all doors that may have been opened to me and my offspring. Seal them with the blood of the Lord Jesus Christ. Amen.

Pause and ask the Lord if there is anything else He would like you to pray or declare, and continue as the Holy Spirit leads you.

Suicidal Tendencies

If you have dealt with suicidal thoughts or attampts at any point in your life or if they have run in your family line, continue praying below.

Prayer of Freedom

Heavenly Father, I _____ confess, repent of and renounce all suicidal thoughts and any attempts I have made to take my own life or injure myself. I confess on behalf of myself and my ancestors for giving place to a spirit of suicide or self-harm. I renounce and reject the lie that life is hopeless and that I can find peace and freedom by taking my own life. I ask you Father to have mercy on my ancestors and me. Please, break every curse of suicide, self-harm, and premature death. I command every spirit of suicide, suicidal thoughts, depression, anxiety, hopelessness, and death to leave me now in the mighty name of Jesus. Lord, I choose to be a good steward of the physical life that You have entrusted to me. In Jesus' name, I pray, Amen.

Pause and ask the Lord if there is anything else He would like you to pray or declare, and continue as the Holy Spirit leads you.

Racism / Chauvinism

If you or your family have participated in racism or chauvinism by action, words or thought, continue praying below.

Prayer of Freedom

Dear Heavenly Father, I know that You love all people equally and that You do not show favoritism. You accept people from every nation who fear You and do what is right. You do not judge them based on skin color, race, economic standing, ethnic background, gender, language denominational preference, or any other worldly matter. I confess on behalf of myself and my ancestors that we have prejudged others or regarded ourselves as superior because of these things. We have been divisive through our attitudes, words, and deeds. I confess, repent of, and renounce all hateful bigotry, chauvinism, pride, and prejudice, and I ask you, Holy Spirit, to close and seal all doors that may have been opened to me and my offspring because of my racism or that of my family. Help me to love all who are created in your image. In the mighty name of Jesus, I break every curse of racism coming down my family line now, and command all evil associated with it to leave and never return, In Jesus name. Amen.

Pause and ask the Lord if there is anything else He would like you to pray or declare, and continue as the Holy Spirit leads you.

Mistreatment of People Groups

An issue that has become even more relevant to us as we have moved to an area with several Native American reservations, is not only the effect that their religions have had on people generationally (see prayer on Native American Spiritualism), but also the effects of how they were treated by other people groups like the early European Americans. This has also brought up the spiritual issue of how the mistreatment of people groups can bring destruction on a group of people or land.

I recommend pausing and reflecting on this issue and asking the Holy Spirit if any of your ancestors have participated in treating other groups of people unfairly. This could be an American and Native American thing. It could be an American and African American thing. It could be an issue of antisemitism in your family line, or bitterness and hatred toward a people group that has been known to have treated your ancestors unfairly. Whatever the situation you may be able to use this prayer as a model and reword it to fit what the Holy Spirit is revealing to you. Ask forgiveness, not only for the practices of your people group that have dishonored the Lord, but also the strife and division between groups of people.

Prayer of Freedom

Father in Heaven, I come to You on behalf of myself and all those in my ancestral line. I ask for Your forgiveness for our sins and rebellion against you. Forgive us for the worship of idols, people, animals, and other things in nature, when that worship should only be to you. Forgive us for ever doing evil in Your name that clearly was not your will. Forgive us for self-righteousness and pride that would cause us to believe that we are better or more valuable than any other group of people that you have created.

Lord, I also come to you as a citizen of the United States, and I ask You to forgive the sins of our forefathers and those that pioneered and settled this land, and the pagan practices, cultures and traditions brought in from foreign lands.

I renounce all statues of false gods, monuments of obelisks and other pagan symbolism, and every graven image that is revered and even worshipped here in this land.

186

On behalf of myself, my generational line, the founding fathers of this nation, and all political leaders in this land, I identify with these sins and the need to acknowledge them to You so that our land may be healed.

I repent on behalf of our political leaders that broke treaties and removed the boundary lines of Native Americans and others to claim them as their own. (Proverbs 22:28) Forgive my people for encroaching on property that didn't belong to us and cheating rightful heirs out of their inheritance. (Proverbs 23:10)

Forgive those who have gone before me for impoverishing Native American families and forcing them out of their homes. Forgive them for making slaves of other races and nationalities and treating humans horribly based on their color, religion, or financial status. Forgive the people of the United States for the grief we caused, the injustices and the bloodshed. Forgive us for broken covenants, vows and agreements and we ask you to break the curses that came as a result of those actions off of our families and our land.

Although, I may not have personally taken part in these sins, I understand that there is a need to recognize the sins of those that came before us and I ask for the blood of Jesus to atone for these things so that this land can be cleansed.

Please allow all those that have been affected by this evil now find the ability to forgive others for generations of mistreatment and injustices. I choose to forgive anyone that I have been offended with. I choose to forgive those that I feel are responsible for my pain or bitterness.

Please let Your restoration be upon us all. I pray for the blessings that have been blocked up, barricaded, unlawfully stolen, hidden or plundered – and I tell them, "Come back into your rightful generational line. Come back into those families and let the blessings flow abundantly in Jesus name."

Pause and ask the Lord if there is anything else He would like you to pray or declare, and continue as the Holy Spirit leads you.

Gossip / Slander / Word Curses

If you or your ancestors have… just kidding. Everyone should pray this prayer.

Prayer of Freedom

Father, I come to You right now in the name of Jesus. I ask You to forgive me and my ancestors for the sin of Loshon Hora, of gossip and slander. I repent of using my mouth to curse others and cause division and discord. I forgive everyone who has gossiped about me and cursed me with their words. I forgive myself for my careless use of words against God, against people, and against myself.

Spirit of gossip, you leave me now. Every spirit of slander and word curses, leave me in the name of Jesus. I come in agreement with the blood of Jesus that the curse is broken and reversed in every area of my life. I command all evil associated with the sins of my mouth and that of my ancestors to leave me now in the mighty name of Jesus.

I renounce every word curse spoken out of my mouth and I break the power of every word curse that has come toward me from others. Lord, help me to control my tongue. I pray that my mouth would be used to declare your will and your words only. In Jesus' name I pray.

Pause and ask the Lord if there is anything else He would like you to pray or declare, and continue as the Holy Spirit leads you.

Word Curses

Pray this prayer to break the power of word curses spoken by you, against you, or both.

Prayer of Freedom

Heavenly Father, I repent on behalf of myself and my ancestors for speaking curses over ourselves or anyone else. I ask you Father to forgive us for any way that we have sinned and created a cause for a curse to come on us or our households.

Ask Holy spirit to reveal any specific sin in this area.

I confess and renounce the sin(s) of _____. I forgive myself and my ancestors for these sins and receive your mercy and forgiveness, Lord. I break all generational curses that have come against my family from the beginning of time to the current generation. I cancel and break every curse of witchcraft. In the mighty name of Jesus, I receive blessing and not curses for me and my offspring. Holy spirit, I ask you to close and seal all doors that have been opened to us through any sins or word curses. I declare that those doors are closed to the enemy and we are cleansed, delivered, healed, and protected by the precious blood of Jesus.

Right now, I declare in Jesus' name, that every curse spoken or unspoken that has come against me and my family: our health, our relationships, our finances, and every other area of life, is broken and reversed in Jesus' name, from this moment on.

Pause and ask the Lord if there is anything else He would like you to pray or declare, and continue as the Holy Spirit leads you.

Pronouncements

Statements or curses that were spoken out over us either by authority figures (parents, teachers, coaches, pastors) or equals (siblings, schoolmates) such as, "you will never amount to anything" or "You are so selfish."

The power of the spoken word has ripple effects in the spiritual realm and an effect of our non-conscious mind, that we may not necessarily see. Science experiments also prove the effect that our words and intentions have on people and other things such as plants, water, etc.

Prayer of Freedom

Heavenly Father, I ask you to forgive me and my ancestors for speaking any word curses or pronouncements over others. I also break the power of every pronouncement spoken over me. I break the pronouncement that _____. I renounce and reject that lie now in Jesus' name.

Ask the Lord for the truth that combats that lie

I declare God's truth that: _____.

Lies of the Enemy

We give the enemy a foothold in our lives when we come into agreement with his lies. Take the time to ask the Lord if there are any lies that you have believed and that you need to renounce. There is power when we use the our words to boldly renounce lies and speak the truth of the Word of God out loud.

Prayer of Freedom

Heavenly Father, I ask you to forgive me and my ancestors for coming into agreement with the deceiving lies of the enemy. I renounce the lie that

_____.

Father, I give you that lie and I ask you to give me Your truth.

Wait and listen for the Lord's response.

In Jesus' name, I declare the truth from my Heavenly Father that _____.

Examples of Truth

Here are some examples of God's truth about us that we can find in His word. I pray that you receive healing as you are led by the Lord, to look these up, study them, and declare them over your life.

I AM ACCEPTED:

John 1:12 - I am God's child.

John 15:15 - I am friend of Jesus.

Romans 5:1 - I have been justified by faith and I'm at peace with God.

1 Corinthians 6:17 - I am united with the Lord and I am one spirit with him.

1 Corinthians 6:19-20 – My body is a temple of the Holy Spirit and I have been bought with a price. I belong to God.

1 Corinthians 12:27 - I am part of the body of Christ.

2 Corinthians 5:21 - I am the righteousness of God in Christ Jesus.

Ephesians 1:5 - I have been adopted as God's child.

Ephesians 2:18 - I have direct access to my Father in Heaven through Jesus and the Holy Spirit.

Colossians 1:14 - I have been redeemed and forgiven of all my sins.

Colossians 2:10 - I am complete in Christ.

I AM SECURE:

Romans 8:1-2 - I am free forever from condemnation.

Romans 8:28 - I am assured that all things work together for good.

Romans 8:31 - I am free from any condemning charges against me.

Romans 8:35 - I cannot be separated from the love of Jesus.

2 Corinthians 1:21-22 - I have been established, anointed and sealed by God.

Colossians 3:3 - I am hidden with Christ in God.

Philippians 1:6 - I am confident that the good work that God has begun in me will be perfected.

Philippians 3.20 - I am a citizen of heaven.

2 Timothy 1:7 - I have not been given a spirit of fear but of power, love and a sound mind.

Hebrews 4:16 - I can find grace and mercy in time of need.

I AM SIGNIFICANT:

Matthew 5:13-14 - I am the salt of the earth and light of the world.

John 15:1-11 - I am a branch of the true vine.

John 15:16 - I have been chosen and appointed to bear fruit.

Acts 1:8 - I am a personal witness of Christ and a host of the power of the Holy Spirit.

1 Corinthians 3:16 - I am God's temple and His Spirit dwells in me.

2 Corinthians 5:17-18 - I am a minister of reconciliation for God.

1 Corinthians 3:9 - I am God's coworker.

Ephesians 2:6 - I am seated with Christ in the heavenly realm.

Ephesians 2:10 - I am God's workmanship, created for good works.

Ephesians 3:12 - I may approach God with freedom and confidence.

Philippians 4:13 - I can do all things through Christ who strengthens me.

Vows

Statements such as "I will never ____." or "I will always _____." are a problem, because they are spoken out of our own will and strength, and many times out of woundedness & sin. We should stay away from any vows or promises made from our soul or flesh or any plans to do anything independently of God. Often what we say we will never do is exactly what happens. Ask the Lord to reveal to you if there are any vows you have made in your own flesh that you need to break the power of.

Prayer of Freedom

In the name of Jesus, ask you Father, to break the vows that I have made out of my own foolishness. Specifically, that __ (list vows) __.

Please cancel all power given to the enemy through my vows, the ones I remember and any unknown vows. I renounce and reject them completely and I now publicly declare and renew my commitment and allegiance to you Father.

I admit that I have spoken the wrong words into existence without realizing their harmful intent. I recognize these words can bring harm spiritually. I now bind my will to the will of My Father in Heaven and His Truth. I break the power of any wrong words I may have spoken, or that others have spoken over me. Help me to have discipline with my words and not use them carelessly. In Jesus' name, Amen.

Pause and ask the Lord if there is anything else He would like you to pray or declare, and continue as the Holy Spirit leads you.

Legalism

Pray this and be free of every religious curse of legalism.

Prayer of Freedom

Father, I ask you to forgive me (and my ancestors) for taking Your grace and law for granted. I ask you to forgive us for seeking righteousness apart from You and what you have done for us. I give You my life, so You may lead me and guide me. I want it to be Your will and Your way in every area of my life.

Father, I ask you in your mercy to break the curse of legalism in my life and in my family line and break every legalistic and religious stronghold of the mind. I confess with my mouth, and believe in my heart that I am saved by grace alone through faith alone. I will serve You with all my heart, because You love me, and not to earn Your love. I break the power of every religious curse that's been on my life and my family right now, in the name of Jesus Christ. I command every religious and legalistic spirit to leave me and my family now and never return.

Father, I ask you to help me and my family to receive the fullness of the intimate relationship that you desire for us to have with you. Teach us how to walk in your grace without abusing it, in Jesus' name. Amen.

Pause and ask the Lord if there is anything else He would like you to pray or declare, and continue as the Holy Spirit leads you.

Not Honoring your father and mother

Ask the Lord if you need to repent of the sin of breaking the 5th commandment by not honoring your father and mother. Then pray below.

Prayer of Freedom

Father, I repent on behalf of myself and my ancestors for any time that we have not honored our father or mother. __Mention any specifics__. I ask you to forgive us for this sin. Thank you for restoring honor and blessing in our relationships. Father, I ask you to break every curse off of my family and me, that was brought on by us not honoring our parents as you have commanded us to do. I command all evil spirits associated with this sin to leave me and my family now and never return. I declare that every curse is broken by the resurrection power of Jesus Christ. I thank you, Lord, that the blessing of long life is ours now in Jesus' name.

Pause and ask the Lord if there is anything else He would like you to pray or declare, and continue as the Holy Spirit leads you.

Financial Strongholds

The curse of poverty

Deuteronomy 28:29
...and you will grope at noon, as the blind man gropes in darkness, and you will not prosper in your ways; but you shall only be

oppressed and robbed continually, with none to save you.

The Blessing of Prosperity

Deuteronomy 28:11
The Lord will make you abound in prosperity, in the offspring of your body and in the offspring of your beast and in the produce of your ground, in the land which the Lord swore to your fathers to give you.

Joshua 1:8
This book of the law shall not depart from your mouth, but you shall meditate on it day and night, so that you may be careful to do according to all that is written in it; for then you will make your way prosperous, and then you will have success.

Matthew 6:33 ESV
But seek first the kingdom of God and his righteousness, and all these things will be added to you.

Prayer of Freedom

I come to You Father, in the name of Jesus. On behalf of myself and my ancestors, I confess and repent of:

__mishandling finances

__stealing or taking more than our share

__being ungrateful for what we did have

__robbing you by withholding tithes and offerings

__not giving when you told us to give whether out of fear or rebellion

__not trusting you to provide for us

__trying to plan our own way and do our own will or business instead of dying to ourselves and following your will for our lives

__using our finances for evil

__impatience and spending money we didn't have when you didn't approve the loan

__using finances to try to earn the approval of others

__judging others who have less or more money than us

__anything else the holy spirit reveals

I forgive my ancestors for the mishandling of finances and the consequences that have come down to me. I forgive myself for any way that I have participated in these sins. I ask you Father for your forgiveness for me and my family.

Cleanse us of all iniquity, and break every curse that has been affecting our finances I pray. According to Your Word and the blood of Jesus. I rebuke the spirit of poverty lack, debt, and failure. All curses are broken and reversed. I receive everything that should have been in my family for generations. I receive now the latter and the former rain. I declare that the enemy will pay back to me and my family 7 times what he has stolen and the Lord will restore to my family all that the locusts have eaten. I receive prosperity and abundance to do the will of the Father.

There will always be enough to do everything that the Lord has called us to do. We are blessed to be a blessing to others around us. Help us to live a life of generosity and steward our finances well. Help us to listen in obedience to You only and not our carnal minds or the enemy, when it comes to financial planning and giving, in Jesus' name! Amen.

Pause and ask the Lord if there is anything else He would like you to pray or declare, and continue as the Holy Spirit leads you.

General Renouncement Prayers

The following are general ministry prayers to keep handy as Holy Spirit reveals any generational sin.

General Sin

Heavenly Father, I confess the sin of my ancestors, and my own sin of _____.

I forgive my ancestors for this sin and for the consequences of the sin that have come down to my family and me. I forgive myself for any way that I have participated in this sin. Lord, I ask you to forgive me and my family for this sin.

In the name of the Lord Jesus Christ, and by the power of His blood, I renounce all evil that has given power to this sin. I ask you Heavenly Father, to cleanse my bloodline from all iniquity and break all curses that have come to us because of it. Please close and seal all doors that may have been opened to me and my offspring.

In the name of Jesus, I sever all evil generational ties from the beginning of time to the current generation, I break every generational curse of

_____ *(name any curse the Holy Spirit reveals)*
and I cast out every demonic spirit associated
with these curses in Jesus' mighty name. All evil
leave me now, leave my family now, and never
return. Father, I ask that You would enable me to
walk by the Spirit and not carry out the desires of
my flesh.

Lord, I humbly ask that you would go deeper and
reveal any other hidden sin that I am unaware of,
in Jesus' name.

*Keep Praying as the Holy Spirit leads you specifically for
your situation. There may be more sin to confess or lies to
renounce. He may lead you to command healing to your
body or soul, command a certain spirit to leave, release a
blessing, or just start praising the Lord.*

Involvement in Questionable Things

Sometimes we can be involved in something that
we are not sure if it was wrong or right.
Sometimes the same act in two different
situations can be safe in one situation and bring a
snare in another. For instance, you can see one
health practitioner that does a certain treatment
based on science and the Lord's design for

healing, but then another practitioner does the same treatment, but using divination and spirit guides. If you have a check in your spirit about something, seek the Lord and repent if necessary.

Prayer of Freedom

Heavenly Father, I confess, renounce and reject my involvement in _____ on behalf of myself and my offspring from now until Jesus returns. I ask you, Holy Spirit, to close and seal all doors that have been opened to me and my offspring. Seal them with the blood of the Lord Jesus Christ. Lord, I ask that you would cleanse me and protect me from all evil. I ask Holy Spirit, that you would give me discernment about the areas in my life that I'm not sure about, in Jesus' name I pray.

Pause and ask the Lord if there is anything else He would like you to pray or declare, and continue as the Holy Spirit leads you.

Active Curses / Witchcraft

This prayer can be said anytime the Holy Spirit reveals to you that witchcraft or cursing is happening toward you.

Prayer of Freedom

In the name of Jesus, I cancel and break every curse of witchcraft, spoken or unspoken, that has come against me or my family. I also break every curse over myself and my family that I have spoken. In the name of Jesus Christ, I claim that not only is the curse broken, but reversed, in Jesus' name. I proclaim right now I am free of every curse. My family members are free of every curse in Jesus' name. Lord, I pray that you would turn every curse intended toward me or my family into a blessing.

Pause and ask the Lord if there is anything else He would like you to pray or declare, and continue as the Holy Spirit leads you.

Breaking Generational Curses

You can go to page 14 for more information about curses and blessings.

The Following Prayer is a sweeping prayer for the breaking of generational curses or iniquities. It is taken from Jubilee Resources International. You can find more like this one at www.JubileeResources.org

Prayer of Freedom

Heavenly Father, creator of heaven and earth, I come to you in the name of the Lord Jesus Christ of Nazareth, your Son.

I come as a sinner seeking forgiveness and cleansing from all sins committed against you, and others created in your image.
I honor my earthly father and mother, and all my ancestors of flesh and blood, adoptive or step parents, but I utterly turn away from and renounce all their ungodly practices, sins and iniquities.

I forgive all my ancestors for the effects of their sins on me and my children.

Thank you, Father, for sending your only Son, the Lord Jesus Christ of Nazareth, to die in my place; to pay the penalty for my sins through His shed blood, and to bear the punishment for the sins and iniquities of my ancestors in His bruised and bleeding body on the Cross of Calvary. Thank you that He is my Holy Scapegoat.

I choose now, to confess and take accountability for the sins through my family bloodlines back to the fourth generation, and to the tenth generation for sexual sins, known and unknown.

I confess and renounce all idolatry, known and unknown, also all involvement with occult power and looking into the hidden things of darkness by my family and ancestors.

In the name of Jesus Christ, I now break and renounce all blood oaths, blood covenants, blood dedications, blood ties and all blood bondages to Satan and any other false gods by my family and myself.

I also cancel all ungodly documents, agreements and assignments against me and my family, past, present and future, and I apply the blood of Jesus Christ to cancel them. I declare their penalty has been paid in full by Jesus at Calvary.

I confess all ungodly behavior, spoken words, thoughts and negative emotions that have had an ill-effect on my family bloodlines, on my marriage and other relationships.

I repent of all word curses spoken over or to others. I release each person from any offence caused, and release my rights to revenge, for the Word of God says that revenge is the Lord's only.

I confess the operation of rejection in my family bloodlines in every form, especially that which is now affecting me, my marriage and my family.

I confess any addictions in my family bloodlines, known or unknown.

I renounce the effects of any untimely death and any effects of war in my family bloodlines. I give to the Lord Jesus Christ all unresolved grief from these deaths, and from death of expectations. I ask you, Lord Jesus, to release me from the consequences of all unresolved grief and disappointments attached to the death of expectations.

I renounce all areas of false guilt and false responsibility in my family bloodlines.

I confess and renounce all religious restrictions and perversion of the Gospel in my family bloodlines, either from a Christian denomination or church, from a different religion, faith or tradition, or from cultic involvement.

I renounce any hereditary illness, whether physical, emotional or mental, and any other weakness in my family bloodlines.

I confess and ask forgiveness for any failure by myself and my ancestors for stealing from God by not bringing to Him our tithes and offerings as His Word commands. This has permitted the Devourer to plunder my family's wealth. I confess this grievous sin and I repent and ask your forgiveness now.

I choose now to be generous, so I break the curse and spirit of poverty off my life now, in the name of Jesus Christ.

I rebuke every related spirit, including greed, covetousness, stinginess, and self-reliance; and I command all such spirits to leave me now harmlessly on my natural breathing, and to go to your appointed place of judgement and not to return to me or my family, in the name of Jesus Christ.

I confess, repent and renounce any and all adultery, fornication, incest, homosexuality or bestiality which has been practiced by me or my family bloodlines.

In the name of Jesus Christ, I now cut off all the effects of these sins, known and unknown, including all ungodly soul ties, and I break every curse involved, in Jesus' name.

I also bind every spirit which empowered these curses and ungodly soul ties, and I command you all to leave me now, and go to your place of appointment to await your judgement in the name of the Lord Jesus Christ

Father God, I come before you in the name of Jesus Christ, confessing these sins and weaknesses which may affect me. I release my ancestors into the freedom of my forgiveness. No longer will I blame them for how I am.

I now lay the punishment and inherited weaknesses on the Lord Jesus Christ of Nazareth, my scapegoat; on His bruised and bleeding body on the cross. I receive your forgiveness and release from their effects.

Thank you, my Lord Jesus Christ of Nazareth, that I can cast my burdens on YOU. Please heal me, renew me and lead me in your ways, that my life may bring glory to your name. Amen

This information is taken from: "Dealing with Costly Words and Actions" by Dr. Selwyn Stevens, (ISBN 978-1877203-742-9) published by Jubilee Resource International Inc., PO Box 36-044, Wellington Mail Centre 5045, New Zealand.

Releasing Generational Blessing

We don't want to just stop at the breaking of curses. Let's actually move forward in declaring blessing over our current family and the generations to come.

Numbers 6:24-26
"The Lord bless you
and keep you;
the Lord make his face shine on you
and be gracious to you;
the Lord turn his face toward you
and give you peace."

Deuteronomy 28:1-17
"Now it shall be, if you diligently obey the Lord your God, being careful to do all His commandments which I command you today, the Lord your God will set you high above all the nations of the earth. 2 All these blessings

213

will come upon you and overtake you if you obey the Lord your God:

3 "Blessed shall you be in the city, and blessed shall you be in the country.

4 "Blessed shall be the offspring of your body and the produce of your ground and the offspring of your beasts, the increase of your herd and the young of your flock.

5 "Blessed shall be your basket and your kneading bowl.

6 "Blessed shall you be when you come in, and blessed shall you be when you go out.

7 "The Lord shall cause your enemies who rise up against you to be defeated before you; they will come out against you one way and will flee before you seven ways. 8 The Lord will command the blessing upon you in your barns and in all that you put your hand to, and He will bless you in the land which the Lord your God gives you. 9 The Lord will establish you as a holy people to Himself, as He swore to you, if you keep the commandments of the Lord your God and walk in His ways. 10 So all the peoples of the earth will see that you are called by the name of the Lord, and they will be afraid of you. 11 The Lord will make you abound in prosperity, in the offspring of

your body and in the offspring of your beast and in the produce of your ground, in the land which the Lord swore to your fathers to give you. 12 The Lord will open for you His good storehouse, the heavens, to give rain to your land in its season and to bless all the work of your hand; and you shall lend to many nations, but you shall not borrow. 13 The Lord will make you the head and not the tail, and you only will be above, and you will not be underneath, if you listen to the commandments of the Lord your God, which I charge you today, to observe them carefully, 14 and do not turn aside from any of the words which I command you today, to the right or to the left, to go after other gods to serve them.

Generational Blessing Prayer

Father God, I thank you for Freedom. I thank you for breaking every generational curse and turning it into a blessing. Help me to store up blessings in Heaven for my future generations, that they may reap the good seeds that I have sown for them.

I declare that me and my offspring are blessed to be a blessing.

We are blessed coming in and blessed going out.

We are blessed in the city, and blessed in the country.

Our offspring are blessed

The produce of our ground is blessed.

Our animals and barns are blessed.

Everything we put our hands to is blessed.

The Lord causes our enemies who rise up against us to be defeated before us; they may come against us one way, but will flee from us seven ways.

The Lord blesses us in the land which He has given us and makes us abound in prosperity.

The Lord will open for us His good storehouse, the heavens, to give rain to our land in its season and to bless all the work of our hands; and we shall lend to many, but borrow from none.

We are the head and not the tail, above, and not below.

Thank you, Lord, for blessing the relationships in our family. I receive healthy marriages, family unity, and blessed friendships for me and my descendants.

I thank you Lord, that we are protected, because we dwell in your shelter and abide under Your shadow, Almighty God.

I declare that we live in divine health and prosper even as our souls prosper. Our bodies are blessed with healing and wholeness, in Jesus' mighty name! Amen

Examples of Spirits

We shouldn't be focused too much on the enemy and his demons, but we shouldn't be ignorant about them either. The following is a list of the names of some spirits, many of which you will find refenced in scripture like, Python, Abaddon, Leviathan, etc. and some are just known to go by a particular name (which is usually just their function). For instance, there is no reference to a spirit of suicide in scripture, but there is a spirit that constantly torments people with suicidal thoughts. It also happens to leave when we tell a spirit of suicide to go, relieving the person of these intrusive thoughts, and so that's just simply what it becomes known as.

This is by no means, an exhaustive list, but just some of the very common spirits driven out in deliverance ministry all over the world. After this list, is an area of the book where we will highlight certain spirits that are well known for the destruction, they cause in the lives of believers along with prayers of renouncement specifically to come out of agreement with that particular spirit.

There may be a spirit that we don't necessarily carry but we may know someone who does, and that spirit is trying to use that person to get to us. When we make sure that there is no unconfessed sin in our lives that is in common with that spirit, it does not have the same power to wreak havoc in our lives. For instance, if we know someone who is acting in a spirit of Jealousy or Control towards us, it is a good idea for us to confess and repent of taking part in the sins of jealousy and control ourselves. This shuts the door on the spirit and breaks its ability to have power in our life through that person. You share your spiritual authority with whatever you come in agreement with. This is why confessing our sin and renouncing these spirits is powerful, because we are declaring that we are coming out of agreement with them. Even though in the past, we gave them a legal right to be in our lives through our unrepentant sin, we are letting them know that our sin is washed in the blood of Jesus and they no longer have authority to be tormenting us.

Some of the following demons are mentioned by name directly in scripture as a demonic spirit. Some are basically just the name of their function. Others are the names of people mentioned in scripture. This will require you to look at scripture through the Hebrew mindset in which it was written, where there are many types and shadows, where certain people or things represent other things. For example, Sarah and Hagar are women mentioned in the Old Testament scriptures, but in Galatians we see that they actually represent the two covenants.

Galatians 4:21-26
"Tell me, you who want to be under law, do you not listen to the law? For it is written that Abraham had two sons, one by the bondwoman and one by the free woman. But the son by the bondwoman was born according to the flesh, and the son by the free woman through the promise. This is allegorically speaking, for these women are two covenants: one proceeding from Mount

Sinai bearing children who are to be slaves; she is Hagar. Now this Hagar is Mount Sinai in Arabia and corresponds to the present Jerusalem, for she is in slavery with her children. But the Jerusalem above is free; she is our mother."

Likewise, there are mentions of false prophets by the name "Jezebel" in both the Old and New Testaments. They are characterized by Control, Manipulation, Intimidation, and leading God's people into immorality and idolatry, and today these spirits who operate in the same way will answer by that same name when being cast out.

Scripture also mentions several times that when the pagan people sacrificed to their idols/gods they were actually sacrificing to the demon spirits that they represent.

Idol worship is demon worship. Things that have been made to look harmless like Greek and Norse mythology are actually demonology. The demon spirits that answer to the names of these gods as they are being cast out have the same characteristics that they are known for in their "mythology."

1 Corinthians 10:19-22 NKJV

"What do I mean then? That a thing sacrificed to idols is anything, or that an idol is anything? **No, but I say that the things which the Gentiles sacrifice, they sacrifice to demons and not to God; and I do not want you to become sharers in demons.** You cannot drink the cup of the Lord and the cup of demons; you cannot partake of the table of the Lord and the table of demons. Or do we provoke the Lord to jealousy? We are not stronger than He, are we?"

Deuteronomy 32:16-17 NASBS
"They made Him jealous with strange gods; With abominations they provoked Him to anger. **They sacrificed to demons, who were not God, to gods whom they have not known,** New gods who came lately, Whom your fathers did not dread."

Psalm 106:35-38 NASBS
"But they mingled with the nations And learned their practices, **And served their idols, Which became a snare to them. They even sacrificed their sons and their daughters to the demons,** And shed innocent blood, The blood of their sons and their daughters, Whom they sacrificed to the idols of Canaan; And the land was polluted with the blood."

Revelation 9:20 NKJV

"But the rest of mankind, who were not killed by these plagues, did not repent of the works of their hands, **that they should not worship demons, and idols of gold, silver, brass, stone, and wood, which can neither see nor hear nor walk.**"

2 Chronicles 11:14-15 NKJV
"For the Levites left their common-lands and their possessions and came to Judah and Jerusalem, for Jeroboam and his sons had rejected them from serving as priests to the Lord. **Then he appointed for himself priests for the high places, for the demons, and the calf idols which he had made.**"

So when we see the names Molech, Baal, or Artemis, etc. These are the demons behind the false gods as mentioned in scripture.

It is also easy to glance over the mentions of the names of spirits in scripture. For instance, we've all heard that "Pride goes before a fall," but did you know that is actually from Proverbs, and they left out the mention of the spirit involved?

Proverbs 16:18 KJV
"Pride goeth before destruction, and a haughty **spirit** before a fall."

The spirit of heaviness/fainting

> "To console those who mourn in Zion,
> To give them beauty for ashes,
> The oil of joy for mourning,
> The garment of praise for the **spirit** of heaviness;
> That they may be called trees of righteousness,
> The planting of the Lord, that He may be glorified."
> Isaiah 61:3 NKJV

Jealousy referred to as demonic:

> James 3:14-16
> "But if you have bitter jealousy and selfish ambition in your heart, do not be arrogant and so lie against the truth. This wisdom is not that which comes down from above, but is earthly, natural, **demonic**. For where jealousy and selfish ambition exist, there is disorder and every evil thing."

Fear/timidity is a spirit:

> 2 Timothy 1:7

For God has not given us a **spirit** of timidity,
but of power and love and discipline.

Jesus asks a demonic spirit its name:

Mark 5:9
"And He was asking him, "What is your
name?" And he said to Him, "My name is
Legion; for we are many."

Common Names/Functions

The following is a list of names that demons go
by. This is by no means an exhaustive list, but just
some examples. Ask the Holy Spirit for the gift of
discernment of spirits to help you know if any of
the following or any other spirits not listed need
to be addressed and told to leave.

- Abaddon/Apollyon
- Absalom
- Abandonment
- Accusation
- Artemis
- Argumentation
- Apathy
- Asmodeus
- Agitation

- Ahab
- Ancestral Spirits
- Animal Spirits
- Antichrist
- Anxiety
- Baal
- Babylonian Spirits/ Pazuzu
- Boastfulness
- Belial

- Baphomet
- Beelzebub
- Betrayal
- Behemoth
- Black Widow
- Cheating
- Cobra/ Black Mamba
- Complacency
- Condemnation
- Control
- Confusion
- Criticism
- Denominational Spirits
- Distraction
- Disobedience
- Discontentment
- Discord
- Division
- Doubt and Unbelief
- Embarrassment
- Envy
- Entitlement
- Exaggeration
- Evasiveness
- Familiar Spirits
- Foolishness
- Fear/ Timidity
- Failure
- Frustration
- Gambling
- Guilt
- Greed
- Gossip
- Haughtiness
- Heaviness/Depression
- Hoarding
- Impatience
- Ignorance
- Irresponsibility
- Idleness
- Infirmity
- Insecurity
- Insomnia
- Jahbulon (Masonry)
- Jealousy
- Jesting
- Jezebel
- Judgementalism
- Legion
- Laziness
- Lilith
- Lust/Perversion
- Lying
- Delilah
- Deception
- Greek Gods/ Goddesses
- Horus
- Kundalini
- Werewolf
- Odin/other Nordic gods
- Orion
- Orphan
- Mammon
- Manipulation
- Misery
- Mockery
- Monitoring Spirits
- Molech/Abortion
- Murder
- Nimrod

- Nightmares
- Paranoia
- Perfectionism
- Procrastination
- Profanity
- Pharisee Spirit
- Poverty
- Pride
- Python / Divination
- Rahab
- Rebellion
- Rejection
- Santeria
- Self-Pity
- Serpent Spirits
- Scorpion Spirits
- Self-harm/Cutting / Mutilation
- Self-Exaltation
- Shame
- Slavery
- Slumber
- Stealing
- Strife
- Stubbornness
- Suicide
- Suspicion
- Torment
- Torture
- Uncleanness
- Ungratefulness
- Vampire
- Vandalism
- Vanity
- Visual Images
- Water/Mermaid Spirits
- Witchcraft
- Worry
- Zozo

Leviathan

There is an entire chapter about this spirit in the Bible and its actually the Lord who is talking about it. Job 41 describes this evil spirit as King over all the sons of Pride. Isaiah 27:1 describes it as a twisting fleeing serpent. It is also mentioned in Job 3:8, Psalm 74:14, and Psalm 104:26. Based on what the Lord warns in Job 41:5-8 and the fact that Bible scholars consider this spirit a high-ranking principality, I do not recommend that you go about confronting this spirit directly by binding it and rebuking it and such. I believe this is a spirit that the Lord defeats for us as we humble ourselves just like the Lord humbled Job who was caught calling himself righteous and rousing Leviathan. Job also received breakthrough when he humbly prayed for his friends even when they weren't treating him well.

Some symptoms that you might be dealing with a spirit of Leviathan

- Twisting of words and confusion
- False accusations
- Prayerlessness
- Jealousy and strife
- Divorce and breaking up of family and friendships
- Sickness in your body
- Offense, especially in ministries

How we open the door to Leviathans attacks:

- Pride and haughtiness
- Self-righteousness
- Offense
- Being too confident in our own ability to do spiritual warfare

Strategies to fight attacks of Leviathan:

- Deep repentance of pride
- Staying humble
- Forgiveness
- Praying for those whom Leviathan is using to wage war against us, our business or our ministry, etc.
- Ask the Lord for strategy in each attack and wait on Him to show you what to do while He fights for you

Prayer of Freedom

Father God, I pray that in your mercy and grace, you would deliver me from the attacks of the spirit of Leviathan. I confess on behalf of myself and my ancestors the sins of pride and self-righteousness. We have been self-seeking and we have done things apart from you that you never asked us to do. Lord, I pray that you would forgive us for these sins. I ask that you would help me to forgive everyone whom Leviathan is using to attack me. I pray Lord that they would be healed, delivered, protected and blessed by you. Father, I come to you in the name of Jesus' my advocate, and I ask you to break every curse of Leviathan that has come down to me either by my own actions or generationally; break every curse Lord and loose every chain. Cleanse us from all iniquity and deliver us from all evil, I pray. Holy Spirit I ask that you would reveal to me anything else that I need to pray about or wait on You for.

Father, I pray that you would give me divine strategy by the power of the Holy Spirit, in how to deal with these attacks and remain free from the torment of evil, in Jesus' name I pray.

Abaddon / Apollyon

Abaddon/Apollyon which means destruction or the Destroyer, is mentioned in Revelation 9:11, Job 28:22, Job 26:6, and Proverbs 27:20

Do you ever feel like you are just working so hard, and no matter what you do, destruction comes to sabotage everything you are trying to accomplish?

Are you bombarded by thoughts of failure? You may want to pray about this.

Prayer of Freedom

Father God, on behalf of myself and my ancestors, I repent of and renounce pride, rebellion, vanity, greed, and double-mindedness that has opened to door to destruction in my life. Lord, I ask you to break every curse, cleanse me of all iniquity and deliver me from all destruction.

I break the power of Abaddon off my life. I bind the spirit of Apollyon from releasing destruction in my life.

I take authority over the enemy that seeks to destroy my peace, my joy, my finances, my relationships, and my calling in Christ Jesus.

I break all curses of destruction in my family and in my bloodline. I declare that I live a life of abundance and shalom peace.

I command mammon, pride, self-destruction and all other destructive spirits to leave me now and never return. I break your hold off my life now in the mighty name of Jesus.

Pause and ask the Lord if there is anything else He would like you to pray or declare, and continue as the Holy Spirit leads you.

Jezebel

Although the Jezebel spirit is represented in the Bible as a woman, it does not actually have a gender. It functions just as well through a man as it does a woman. The following are some characteristics of a Jezebel spirit.

- Control through many strategies
- Manipulation and Intimidation
- Flips back and forth between flattery and intimidation
- Idolatry and leading others into idolatry
- Sexual power
- Takes credit for everything
- Volunteers for things as a means of control
- Talks in many words to bring confusion
- Lies intentionally and with a straight face
- Competitive, Jealous, and envious
- Pushy and domineering
- False prophetic gifting
- Sowing seeds of discord
- Thrives off truces and treaties
- Hates godly authority and does not submit to it, but will try to put themselves in a position right next to a leader as their "second in command" "assistant" or "armor bearer" as a means to control them

- Tries to make the innocent look like the trouble maker
- Knows it all and doesn't want to hear any other sides of an issue
- Gives gifts publicly and with strings attached
- Religious and usually finds its way into the church
- Hides well and will wait patiently for an opportune time to control and manipulate through that person again

Jezebel is a known enemy of prophetic people and church leaders. It hates and targets true prophets of the Lord. It will try to control Pastors and leaders. Pastors and leaders that have anything in common with an Ahab spirit are easy for Jezebel to influence. Prophets who have anything in common with Jezebel are an easy target. Some signs and symptoms that you may be dealing with a Jezebel spirit attacking your life are.

- Insomnia and extreme fatigue
- Fear and anxiety
- Discouragement and dread
- Depression and suicidal thoughts
- Greater sexual temptation
- Frequent and unusual sicknesses
- Frequent and unusual accidents
- Constant false accusations

- Idolatry (looking to things for joy)

It is important that you give a person acting in a Jezebel spirit a chance to repent, but if they don't you will need to let them go. Stop allowing them to elevate themselves in the organization and influence you in any way.

Prayer of Freedom

Father, I acknowledge that my ancestors and I have yielded ourselves to the spirit of Jezebel. I ask You to forgive me and my ancestors for our tolerance of the Jezebel spirit. Please forgive me for every way I have opened myself up to this spirit. Help me to reject every type of this thinking and the desire to control and manipulate other people. On behalf of myself and my ancestors, I confess and repent of:

_ Opposing Your prophets & ordained authority
_ Satisfying my own ego
_ Dominating, intimidating and manipulating
_ Opposing the work of the Holy Spirit
_ Obstructing the flow of Your Spirit
_ Idolatry in all its forms
_ Discouraging others from obeying You
_ Witchcraft, rebellion and controlling behavior

_ Walking after the desires of the flesh
_ Evoking the Ahab spirit in others
_ Allowing a spirit of Ahab to influence me
_ Abusing my authority and leadership
_ Twisting other peoples' words to make myself look good
_ Distorting Your words, or giving false prophetic words knowingly or unknowingly
_ Lies and underhandedness
_ Falsely accusing or putting blame or suspicion on others
_ Stubbornness, pride, arrogance and argumentativeness
_ Criticism, lies, and tearing down of others
_ Ignoring the warnings of the Holy Spirit
_ Sexual immorality including sexual power or manipulation through sex
_ Following tradition instead of revelation, and legalism instead of the Holy Spirit
_ Trying to control others through a religious mask, knowledge, secretiveness, works, long and empty prayers, 'unique' experiences and super-spirituality
_ Anger outbursts and creating confusion
_ Stepping on people to get what I wanted.

Father, I ask for forgiveness for all these sins that me and my ancestors have committed. I forgive my ancestors and myself for these sins and I forgive everyone who has allowed Jezebel to use them to attack me in any way. Forgive them Lord for they know not what they are doing. I ask you to block any transfer of this spirit to my children and descendants. Let this curse stop with me. I renounce and bind every spirit of Jezebel that has influenced me or my family in any way, and I pull down this stronghold in my life. Help me Lord, to live by Your standard of righteousness, holiness and conduct and help me to walk in humility and truth. In Jesus' Name.

Lord, I ask you to cleanse my bloodline of all iniquity. Break every Jezebelic curse off of my family and me. I ask you Lord to heal every person whom I have caused pain while allowing this spirit to influence my actions.

I break all agreements with the spirit of Jezebel in the name of Jesus. I plead the blood of Jesus against this wicked power. I renounce the theology, tactics, and temptations of the Jezebel spirit. Cleanse me of all unrighteousness that this spirit has brought into my life. I ask you lord that you would continue to heal me of all wounds of rejection and any other things that Jezebel might try to use as an opportunity in my life.

I renounce all soul ties with Jezebel. I renounce all partnerships with Jezebel. I ask you Lord to show me how I was deceived so that I don't fall for the tactics of Jezebel again. I renounce every spirit of rejection, control, intimidation, manipulation, idolatry, Ahab, and any other spirit related to Jezebel. I now bind and rebuke the spirit of Jezebel from my life. Every evil spirit must leave me now and never return. Holy Spirit, I ask that you close every door that was opened to Jezebel in my life, and seal them with the blood of Jesus.

Pause and ask the Lord if there is anything else He would like you to pray or declare, and continue as the Holy Spirit leads you.

Ahab

Where there is Jezebel, there is usually an Ahab spirit at work as well. I have found that most people have to guard themselves from being deceived by one more than the other, depending on our calling, gifting, and personality type.

Jezebel seeks to control, intimidate and manipulate. Ahab is more of a passive spirit that does anything to keep Jezebel happy and avoid confrontation, even at the expense of tolerating evil and being heavily influenced by Jezebel's tactics. Ahab was one of the most wicked Kings of Israel.

Signs of an Ahab spirit:
- Carelessness and irresponsibility
- Codependency
- Passive aggression
- Passivity, letting others handle problems that they should be handling themselves
- Vanity and fragile ego
- Being deceived or seduced into idolatry and sin
- Sexual addictions and lust of the flesh
- Constant battle of being controlled and resisting control
- Manipulation and being manipulated
- Outbursts of anger
- Being sucked into Jezebel's battles with Prophets
- Impulsiveness
- Weak will
- Empty words and empty promises

In relationships: The spouse or family member of someone with a controlling or dominating temperament is a target of an Ahab spirit. Relationships like this are a constant battle of control or be controlled; manipulate or be manipulated. Emotional outbursts are frequent it's a constant roller coaster of fighting and making up only to fight again.

In Ministry: Pastors are often the target of an Ahab spirit, because they love people and want to care for their flock. They want people to like them and they want to keep people happy, and keep the church together. If they aren't careful, this can lead to passivity and a tolerance of evil when it should be dealt with.

Father God, I confess on behalf of myself and my ancestors that we have allowed the spirit of Ahab to work through us. We have been passive and irresponsible. Forgive us Lord for satisfying our own ego and vane ambitions. I repent of and renounce all lust, and sexual sin, all codependency and tolerance of evil.

Forgive me Lord for double-mindedness, and making empty promises. Help me to be a person of my word. Help me to be bold in the face of evil and stand for truth. I renounce the spirit of Ahab and all its cohorts. I renounce all fear of confrontation, manipulation, angry outbursts, and pride. I come out of agreement with the spirit of Jezebel and all its strategies and deceptions.

Forgive me Lord for tolerating the Jezebel spirit to try to keep the peace. I now know that it only ends in disobedience and destruction. Lord, cleanse my bloodline of all iniquity and break every curse. I ask that in your mercy, You would deliver me from all evil. I refuse to be dominated controlled or deceived. I break every curse of Ahab and Jezebel right now, in Jesus' name! Father, open my spiritual eyes and help me see the ways I have been deceived, so that I don't fall for it anymore. Holy Spirit fill me from the top of my head to the soles of my feet. I ask you now for the gift of discernment of spirits. Help me to have wisdom. Help my "yesses" mean yes and my "no's" mean no. I pray that you would break every curse of anger and impulsiveness off me and my bloodline. Help me be disciplined in my words and actions. In Jesus' name I pray.

Pause and ask the Lord if there is anything else He would like you to pray or declare, and continue as the Holy Spirit leads you.

Death

Signs of attacks from a spirit of death:
- Family history of untimely death
- Miscarriages

- Fear of death
- Suicidal thoughts
- Severe and deadly illness

Prayer of Freedom

Heavenly father, I repent to You this day for any inner vow I have made or willful sin that opened the door to a spirit of death. I acknowledge that this vow is a lie and does not line up with Your Word or Your character. I repent of all words and actions from me that have reinforced the effects of this vow. I repent of all thoughts and attempts of suicide and self-destructive behavior

In Jesus' name, I renounce every vow and every action on my part or by any of my former generations, that have opened the door to a spirit of death or the spirit of suicide. Spirit of death, I declare that you can no longer use these lies against me. I shut the door on you. I choose life. I renounce all lies that I have believed about myself and choose to accept the truth of God's Word.

In the name of Jesus, I now break the power of the spirit of death and suicide over my life, and all generational influences that have given it any power. The affect and rule of every spirit of death and suicide is canceled now. I command you to leave me now in the powerful name of Jesus.

I break every word curse that has been spoken over me. I bind all witchcraft that has come against me, in Jesus' mighty name.

I come against every death spirit and bind you in the name of the Lord Jesus. I take authority over you in the name of Jesus and I command you to leave me now.

I will live and not die and declare the works of the Lord! With long life my Lord satisfies me. My God still has work for me to do here on this earth, and I will live my purpose in divine health until the time He has appointed for me.

Pause and ask the Lord if there is anything else He would like you to pray or declare, and continue as the Holy Spirit leads you.

Infirmity

Ask the Holy spirit to reveal any open doors to a spirit of infirmity in your life. Confess all known generational sin. Ask the lord to break every curse of sickness that has come down to you through the generations. Then use your power and authority in Jesus Christ to kick those spirits of sickness out of your life.

Prayer of Freedom

Heavenly Father, I thank you that by Jesus' stripes I am healed. I come against every spirit of infirmity and bind you in the name of the Lord Jesus. I renounce every medical diagnosis that has given any demons legal authority in my life. I break the power of every word curse spoken over my life and over my health.

Body, I command you to line up with the word of God and His perfect design for my health. I command every cell in this body to properly function as it was designed to do. Sickness must leave my body now In Jesus' name. Every demonic spirit of sickness and infirmity, you must leave me now, in the mighty name of Jesus.

Ask the Holy Spirit for the gift of discernment to know what sickness or spirit to tell to leave. Here are some examples:

-Cancer
-Arthritis

-Allergies
-Auto Immune Disorder

- Food Allergies
- Blood Disorders
- Thyroid Disease
- Vaccine Injury
- Migraines
- Stroke
- Heart Disease
- Fibromyalgia
- Infertility
- Deaf /Dumb Spirit
- Skin Conditions
- Gout
- Stomach Issues
- Gallbladder
- Turrets
- Diabetes
- Scoliosis/Back Problems
- Ulcers
- Paralysis
- Tinnitus
- Vertigo
- Fatigue
- Seizures
- Epilepsy
- Crohn's Disease
- Lupus
- Asthma
- COPD
- Acid Reflux
- Restless Leg Syndrome
- Endometriosis
- IBS
- Tumors/Cysts
- PCOS
- Deformity
- Pain
- Sinus Pressure
- Spasms
- Blindness
- Lyme Disease
- Insanity
- Schizophrenia
- PTSD
- Trauma
- Alzheimer's
- Dementia
- Autism
- Multiple Personality Disorder
- Bipolar Disorder
- Dyslexia
- Hallucinations
- Numbness
- OCD
- Disorder

Extra Help and Prayers

Jewish Participants

Matthew 27:25
Let the responsibility for his death fall on us
and on our children.

Prayer of Freedom

In the Name of my Messiah Jesus Christ, I cancel
all rights over ancestors through cursing that have
affected me. I confess on behalf of myself and my
ancestors that we have used our mouth to speak
curses over ourselves and others. I ask you
forgive us Father God, and break every word
curse that has come against me and my family
line. I declare blessing over my family in Jesus'
name.

Continue as the Holy Spirit Leads.

The Truth About Our Heavenly Father

Sometimes in order to receive the fullness of
everything the Lord plans for us, we have to come
to a place where we truly believe that He is our
perfect Father, who loves us unconditionally.

Depending on how your experience has been with your father here on earth, this may be hard to receive. If your earthly father has been abusive or even not present at all, it may be difficult to understand and receive the perfect Love of our Heavenly Father. We can be non-consciously filtering this relationship through our pain or disappointment.

If this sounds like an area you may struggle in, I encourage you to close your eyes and picture our Heavenly Father. What do you see? How could this image of Him be distorted through your view of your dad here on earth?

Prayer of Freedom

Heavenly Father, I forgive my earthly dad for _____, and how it made me feel _____. I repent for thinking that you would treat me the same way. I ask Father, that You would heal every wound in my soul that was caused by my dad's failure to _____.

This would be a good time to close your eyes again and picture how you see your Father in Heaven. Does He look different? Ask the Lord if there is still something blocking you from receiving His love and pray through that again as He leads.

Note: You can also pray through this in a similar way with how you see or receive the Holy Spirit and also Jesus. Many times, we filter how we see or receive the Holy Spirit based off of our relationship with our mom and our view of Jesus can sometimes be distorted by pain from relationships with siblings or peers. I encourage you to just wait on the Lord a bit, and ask Him if there is something that He wants to heal you of or deliver you from in this area.

Below are some helpful affirmations to speak.

Renounce / Announce

I renounce the lie that my Heavenly Father is distant, uninterested or too busy for me.

I announce the truth that My Heavenly Father is knows me intimately. His heart yearns for me and He wants to be involved in every part of my life. (Psalm 139:1-18, Jeremiah 31:20, Ezekiel 34:11-16, Hebrews 13:5)

I renounce the lie that my Heavenly Father is insensitive, impatient, and always angry with me.

I announce the truth that My Heavenly Father is compassionate and gracious, slow to anger and abounding in loving kindness. (Psalm 103:8-14, Exodus 34:6, 2 Peter 3:9)

I renounce the lie that my Heavenly Father is mean and demanding.

I announce the truth that My Heavenly Father is Accepting and loving. He rejoices over me with joy. (Zephaniah 3:17, Romans 15:7)

I renounce the lie that my Heavenly Father is cruel, or passive and cold.

I announce the truth that My Heavenly Father is Warm and affectionate. He handles me gently and I am safe in His protection (Isaiah 40:11, Hosea 11:3-4, Psalm 18:2, Jeremiah 31:3, Isaiah 42:3)

I renounce the lie that my Heavenly Father wants to make my life miserable.

I announce the truth that My Heavenly Father is Trustworthy and wants to give me a full life; His will is good, perfect and acceptable. (Lam. 3:22-23, John 10:10, Romans 12:1-2)

I renounce the lie that my Heavenly Father is Controlling or manipulative.

I announce the truth that My Heavenly Father is Full of grace and mercy. He gives me freedom to fail. (Luke 15:11-16, Hebrews 4:15-16)

I renounce the lie that my Heavenly Father is condemning or unforgiving.

I announce the truth that My Heavenly Father is compassionate and forgiving; His arms are open to embrace me when I run to Him. (Psalm 130:1-4, Luke 15:17-24)

Cleansing & Blessing Home and Land

Our homes should be a sanctuary for our family to live in and worship the Lord. It should be a place filled with the manifest presence of God and His perfect peace. Sometimes when our home doesn't feel that way, it is because evil has crept in somehow. Ask the Holy Spirit if there is anything in your home that does not honor the Lord and is possibly opening the door for the enemy to come in. It is a good idea to go room by room and ask the Lord to highlight anything that should not be in your home and reveal to you anything that happened in that room that you may need to renounce. If the Lord shows you things to get rid of (there's quite a list in the witchcraft section and false religion section of this book) I recommend that you burn what you can and chuck anything else in a dumpster. Whatever you do, make sure it leaves your property completely and you're not just selling or giving it to someone else to deal with the spiritual consequences.

You have legal right to do this at any property, home or apartment that you own or rent. Also, if you run a business, own other land, or lead an organization like a church, the leadership has a right to do this.

It is best if the head of the household or business or church is involved in this process as they are in the best position of spiritual authority there. With that being said, I believe there is grace in special situations where maybe the head of the household isn't a believer, and the wife or daughter wants to still pray, and maybe invite a church leader to pray with her. Be led by the Holy Spirit in this.

Also, if you have a right to be staying in a room, whether it be a hotel room or at someone's home or rental, you can anoint that room and pray over it. As far as the rest of the home or hotel that you don't have dominion in at the time, there is only so much you can do. After several interesting experiences staying in different places, we've learned to always cleanse the room we are staying in right away, by the power of Jesus. It has made such a big difference in our stays and how well we sleep.

I definitely do not recommend ever marching around someone else's home or business or trying to cleanse something that is not yours. I'm not saying the Lord wont ever ask someone to do something like that in a very rare occasion, but in most cases, you would just be picking fights with spiritual entities that were outside of the dominion of authority that the Lord has given you.

When you pray, you can walk completely around your property line, praying and applying the blood of Jesus by faith. We have even poured anointing oil on the corners of our property. Some people will write scriptures on wooden stakes and put them in the ground. Be led of the Lord in this. Our faith is not in the oil or other symbols and actions, it is in the power of God, but there is something to be said about anointing with oil and prophetically using symbols and objects to dedicate dwellings and land. Scripture is full of examples of this.

Confession of the Sins on the Property

Lord I ask forgiveness on behalf of ourselves, this land and home, and anyone who has dwelled here before us for any:

- idolatry, witchcraft, occult activity, sorcery, satanic worship, or dark arts of any kind
- dedications to false gods, idols, or curses placed.
- sexual sins or perversions
- shedding of innocent blood, violence, murder, or criminal activity
- ungodly covenants or oaths
- breaking of godly covenants or agreements
- substance abuse

- strife, fighting, divorce, family alienation, or bickering
- racism or anti-Semitism
- persecution of the righteous
- ungodly entertainment of any kind
- evil words spoken

In the name of Jesus, I command every evil spirit to leave this property and home. I break every curse and cancel any legal rights that any evil has had to this home or land. Lord, we dedicate this land completely to You. Let it be used for Your glory and Yours alone. I bring this property under the blood of Jesus. I ask you, Father, to release your angels to protect this property and all who dwell here. Holy Spirit you are welcome to come, fill every part of this Land, and manifest your presence here. Father, may only Your will be done on this land from here on out. Help us be good stewards of it I pray in Jesus' name.

Vehicles

You can anoint your vehicles with oil and do anything else symbolically that the Lord leads you to do.

Psalm 91:10 "No disaster will come near you, and no plague or disaster near your dwelling." May the

Lord keep this vehicle and all who are in it from any wrecks, break downs, vandalism, theft, or any other harm. May it be a carriage of pleasant conversations, anointed prayer times, learning the word of God, and spiritual growth. I pray Lord that you would send angels to always protect this vehicle and everyone in it. Bring it safely from destination to destination, in Jesus' name.

Blessing to speak:

May the Lord bless this home, land, and every building on it to be a sanctuary of rest, renewal, and refreshing.

May it be a haven of God's perfect peace and a place of unity, harmony, and submission to Godly authority.

May the sounds of joy and laughter be heard here as people continually love and enjoy each other in the presence of the Lord.

May this be a place of unconditional love and continual outpouring of the Holy Spirit.

May this property and home be a place where many are born again, healed, delivered, and discipled in Jesus Christ.

May many be baptized in the Holy Spirit and receive impartation from Jesus here.

May this be a place where the things of God are loved and revered and Word of God is honored and obeyed.

May you be holy ground of praise, worship, prayer, and intercession done in Spirit and truth.

May this home be a place of sweet rest and pleasant dreams. In this place, shall the direction of God's will be learned and revealed. May dreams and visions from God, and the gifts of the Holy Spirit flow in this place, bringing direction, revelation, and truth. May all the inhabitants of this home, and their relatives, and friends enjoy supernatural peace and safety from all acts of violence, including break-ins, theft, fire, and storm. May they find sweet rest and sense the Lord's presence always on this property, in Jesus' name.

Anointing and Blessing Home

You can symbolically place the blood of Jesus on the front door frame, symbolizing the Blood of the Passover lamb, Jesus, or you can anoint them with oil; whatever you feel led by the Lord to do.

Declaration

I declare that the _____ family are overcomers by the Blood of the Lamb of God and the word of their testimony. I speak that this home has a hedge of protection around it, and no curse can rest on it. All evil must pass over it not bringing any harm to it or anyone in it, in Jesus' name.

Rooms of Home

You can also anoint doorframes and windows with oil or some sort of symbol of the blood of Jesus.

In bedrooms: I speak blessings of restful sleep and protection. Let this be a room where pleasant and helpful dreams from the Lord are experienced, in Jesus' name.

Psalm 3:5 "I lay down and slept; I awoke, for the Lord sustains me."

Psalm 4:8 "I will both lie down in peace and sleep, for you alone, O Lord, make me dwell in safety."

Psalm 127:2 "The Lord gives to His beloved, even in their sleep."

This is where you may want to pray more specifically about each person who sleeps in each room. You can pray for protection over the marriage bed if applicable, or against fear if someone had been having nightmares, etc.

In bathrooms: May this room be a blessed place to prepare for the day, as well as prepare for rest at night. I pray this would be a place where we trust in the Lord with all our hearts and acknowledge Him in all our ways so that He straightens our path. (Proverbs 3:5-6)

Continue praying specifically about the bathroom according to specifics about your family and whatever the Lord inspires you to pray.

In the Kitchen: I bless this space with pleasant conversation and God's presence. May god give our family provision and strength for the word of God says, Exodus 23:25 "So shall you serve the Lord your God and he will bless your bread and your water; and I will take sickness away from the midst of you." Thank You Lord, for blessing our kitchen and everything in it, I ask you to bless and sanctify all food and water coming through it. I pray that we will always be overflowing with an abundance of food for our family. Help us to have healthy eating habits, and glorify You in how we feed Your temple.

Pause and listen to the Lord for anything else that He would like to pray or declare over the space.

In the living room(s): Joshua 24:15 "As for me and my house, we will serve the Lord." May the Lord bless this room with God honoring fellowship, singing and praise, and sharing testimonies of God's goodness."

Continue according to the specifics of what your family does most in this room, do you homeschool? Lead Bible study? Have family time? Be specific about what you believe the Lord's will is for that room.

In the entryway/hallways: May the Lord bless our going out and our coming in and may we acknowledge him in all our ways, and He will direct our paths. Thank you, Lord, for peace and safety in this space. I pray that as people walk in to our home, they will immediately sense Your peace.

Pause and listen to the Lord for anything else that He would like to pray or declare over the space.

Office: May this space be used mightily for the glory of God. I pray that new ideas would flow. I pray for a sound mind in this place. I pray, Lord, that you would bless all business and activity done here. Help us to be good stewards of all you have given us, and I pray that you will increase our territory as we walk in obedience to You.

Pause and listen to the Lord for anything else that He would like to pray or declare over the space.

A few other things you can anoint and pray blessing over

Check book (representing your finances): Proverbs 10:22 "It is the blessing of the Lord that makes rich, And He adds no sorrow to it." May the Lord rebuke the devourer for our sake, open the heavens above, and give us great prosperity and abundance for we are tithers and give in

258

obedience to the Lord. May raises and bonuses and increase come to our family. Thank You Lord, for blessing and protection over our finances, in Jesus' name.

Pause and listen to the Lord for anything else that He would like you to pray or declare over your finances.

Animals: Psalms 24:1 "The earth is the Lord's, and all it contains, the world, and those who dwell in it." May the Lord bless you with long healthy lives and all to go well with you. May you have favor and be a joy to us. The Lord set you apart unto him as holy so nothing evil can touch you. I bless you in Jesus' name.

Pause and listen to the Lord for anything else that He would like you to pray or declare over your animals.

Gateways: You can specifically anoint any access points that the enemy might try to use to get into your home whether through media, a person, witchcraft, etc. This includes TVs, Computers, phones, mirrors, back/side doors, windows etc. and pray over them specifically as led by the Lord.

Closing prayer

Father God, we dedicate all we have to you and ask You to set it apart as holy. We ask you to send your angels to watch over it and protect it. Let no evil come near us. This is Your property, Lord. We pray that Your will be done on it and in it and with it, in Jesus name we pray, Amen.

Notes:

The Lord inhabits the praises of His people and the enemy hates it. I recommend making your home a place of worship and praise. Be watchful about what makes its way into your house, especially if you have kids. People will give you gifts all the time and many mainstream toys and games are just evil wrapped up in a cute package.

There is no set schedule of how often you should cleanse or bless your home and land. This isn't a religious ritual, so just be led of the Lord. If you sense that something just isn't right after you have guests over or something significant happens, then go ahead and pray over it again. We don't want to ever fall into the trap of ritualistically cleansing our house out of fear, but we also don't want to ignore when something isn't right and be tolerant of evil in any way.

Made in the USA
Las Vegas, NV
21 November 2024

12237044R00163